THE LIMIT

THE LIMIT

ENGINEERING ON THE BOUNDARIES OF SCIENCE

MIKE DASH

This book is published to accompany the television series entitled *The Limit* which was first broadcast in 1995.

Published by BBC Books
an imprint of BBC Worldwide Publishing,
BBC Worldwide Ltd, Woodlands, 80 Wood Lane,
London W12 0TT

First published 1995
© Mike Dash 1995

The moral right of the author has been asserted

ISBN 0 563 37117 X

Designed by Hammond Hammond
Maps on pages 16 and 43 by Simon Roulstone

Set in Garamond Simoncini by Selwood Systems, Midsomer Norton
Printed and bound in Great Britain by Butler & Tanner Ltd, Frome, Somerset
Colour separations by Radstock Repro, Midsomer Norton
Jacket printed by Lawrence Allen Ltd, Weston-super-Mare

ACKNOWLEDGEMENTS

I am grateful for the help of the production team responsible for the BBC Television series *The Limit*, particularly that of the producers, Martin Mortimore, Saul Nasse and Emma Swain. The engineers who beat the many limits described in this book provided both inspiration and practical advice; they also saved me from more errors than I care to remember. The London Library proved, as ever, an invaluable resource. It goes without saying that I am also indebted to my wife, Penny, whose own limits were tested, but not found wanting, by this project.

Note: In accordance with general engineering practice this book uses mainly metric measurements. Imperial measures are used in historical contexts and given in brackets for dimensions where they are the official system.

PICTURE CREDITS

Go back 400 years to Leonardo da Vinci's sketch of a helicopter, or further back to the Romans and their central heating or the Greek machines of war, and it becomes clear: human beings have always extended their power and abilities by combining a knowledge of physical principles with a hefty dose of imagination. If there are limits, they are not in the mind. So why did it take so long to lift the helicopter off the drawing board? And why do central heating systems still work in much the same way as they did in ancient Rome?

It is not enough for engineers to *understand* physical principles – how a wing flies or why hot air rises. They must also find the right materials, generate sufficient power and, crucially, develop ways to control the machines they design. And that is what this book is about: the visionaries – past and present – who have organized energy and materials so that we can build bigger, go further, travel faster. By looking at some of them and the barriers they have broken, we hope to learn what engineering is about and, perhaps, what makes engineers tick.

Engineering has always changed lives, but never more rapidly than today. Ironically, this means that modern engineers receive less public recognition than their predecessors. The rate of change is so fast that we often take new breakthroughs for granted. The gasps of amazement are fewer now than they were in the Victorian era when record-breaking bridges, trains and ships made national celebrities out of pioneers like Thomas Telford, George Stephenson and Isambard Kingdom Brunel. The great achievements of the past seem all the more romantic because they were the work of dedicated individuals, led by vision and fired by passion. Somehow they seem to have been more in touch with their projects, holding a slide-rule in one hand and scribbling equations with the other. Today, high-powered computer programs can solve many of the equations, and even come up with the designs. However, there are still people of vision and imagination who can push back boundaries and break the limits in their own territory.

ENGINEERING

Big ideas need major planning and of the projects, only two are really under way: Hugh Doherty's Jubilee Line Extension tunnel in London and Niels Gimsing's Storebaelt bridge in Denmark. The others are still being designed, drawn and simulated in every conceivable way. For the engineer who is breaking new ground, there is always an element of uncertainty – lessons from the past, which crop up throughout these pages, are often reminders of what can go wrong.

When engineering theory does take on physical form, it often starts as a small-scale model that is submitted to wind-tunnel tests, sea-keeping tests or strength tests. But every model is a compromise; the forces that act at a small scale are seldom a true reflection of the real thing. For Jean-Jacques Huber's super-jumbo aircraft for instance, a scale-model plane will only give really accurate results in scale-model air where the molecules are closer packed than normal air. To mimic this, the latest wind tunnels are supplied with very low temperature air at high pressure.

When the design of a major project is complete, there is a final hurdle before construction begins: persuading the customer to find the funds. Engineers today must also be salesmen. Niels Gimsing spent years persuading the Danish authorities to fund his record-breaking bridge; and David Giles has spent as much time exhorting industry to back his high-speed cargo ship as he has on its design.

When the building stage is finally reached engineers are usually familiar with the materials they are working with – whether steel, concrete or carbon fibre. But even this is not certain: in New York and Milan two rival engineers, Stephen Gorevan and Mauro Fenzi, are working in the realms of the truly unknown. They are competing to come up with an automatic robot to sample a distant comet that could have the consistency of anything from shaving foam to granite.

Of all the limits that face an engineer perhaps the most important are the constraints imposed by the rest of us. Anyone who lives near an airport would have a view about a new super-jumbo aircraft, and it would be hard for city dwellers to ignore Keizo Shimizu's Millennium Tower. Ultimately, we should all feel some responsibility for the major projects described in this book, even if we also accept them as the dreams of six of today's limit-busting engineers.

Martin Mortimore
Series Producer, *The Limit*

AT THE LIMIT

CHAPTER ONE

LONG

J ames Lawson, wine merchant of Dundee, Scotland, stood on the embankment outside his home and gazed out into the wildest storm he could remember. The wind tore down the Firth of Tay, whipping the waters into a frenzy of foam and whitecaps, and blew through the streets of Magdalen Green so fiercely that people on their way to church had the greatest difficulty in forcing their way across the street. But Lawson's eyes were on the river, and on the waves that crashed against the girders of the great railway bridge that spanned the firth from St Fort to Magdalen Point. It was a quarter past seven on the evening of Sunday, 28 December 1879, and a train was pushing its way over the crossing.

The train was the 5.20 from Burntisland – a locomotive, five carriages and a guard's van belonging to the North British Railway company and was conveying passengers and the evening mails to the Scottish port. On board, scattered among the commercial travellers, families returning from visits to relatives and tradesmen home from a weekend away, sat no fewer than five passengers wearing mourning dress for members of their families. Soon those families would be mourning them too, for as the train entered the central section of the bridge, a lattice tunnel of thirteen 'high girders' that rose more than 78 feet above the Tay, Lawson saw two streams of fire cascade down into the river, and two great geysers of water rise momentarily above the broken surface then subside.

Much later, giving evidence to a board of inquiry into the events of that evening, he recalled that he had turned to a friend standing beside him and yelled over the wind: 'There is a train into the river!'

In truth, the men could not be certain what had happened. It was very dark; the storm had all but blotted out the moon, which peered out only occasionally from between the racing clouds, and it was hard to see the 2 miles across the estuary. But they were sure enough to run to Tay Bridge Station, where they found stationmaster James Smith.

'We have seen fire falling from the bridge, Mr Smith,' Lawson remembered gasping. 'We are very much afraid it's down.'

Smith went out into the storm, and walked along the platform and up the line, where he found locomotive foreman James Roberts. Roberts had discovered that the signals that warned of trains approaching over the bridge had failed, and was

Previous page: The West Bridge, part of the Storebaelt crossing.

searching for the fault when the stationmaster arrived. 'The wires are down,' Smith told him. 'The bridge is down. We must go out along the bridge, for no one knows what has happened.' They went, walking upright at first, then crawling. Fierce gusts pressed against them, and the men feared they would be blown into the river. They lay down on their stomachs; Smith could feel the girders move beneath him and he was afraid. 'I can go no further,' he called to Roberts, 'I'm too giddy.'

But foreman Roberts pressed on, squirming on his stomach for nearly a kilometre, until he saw a break in the bridge ahead of him. He inched up to the chasm, where the bent and broken tracks pointed down to the river, and peered towards the far bank. At last the moon came out and he could see that Lawson had been

All seventy-five people on the 5.20 p.m. train from Burntisland to the Scottish port of Dundee were burned, crushed or drowned when, at the height of the fiercest storm in living memory, the flimsy Tay Bridge collapsed into the river.

right. There was a gap, a huge gap nearly 1200 yards across, in the bridge where the thirteen high girders had once stood.

James Lawson had witnessed the supreme disaster of the railway age: the end of the Tay Bridge and the death of seventy-five passengers on the North British Railway. Yet, during its short life, the bridge had been widely regarded as one of the wonders of its age. Though functional rather than beautiful in construction, and conventional rather than innovative in design, it exceeded the limits set by all its predecessors. It was the first bridge to stretch more than a mile, and the railway line that ran across it was supported by no fewer than eighty-five wrought-iron piers, each made of six huge pipes cross-braced to lend support to the structure. The bridge curved out in an arc and then crossed the river diagonally, sticking to a route chosen so that its pylons could rest, so far as was possible, on solid rock; as a result it was all but 2 miles long from end to end. It was also narrow and flimsy and built of indifferent iron that was full of cracks and crevices. After it had been opened in the spring of 1878, workmen spoke of finding rivets forced out by the swaying of the girders and railway passengers swore their carriages rocked alarmingly when the wind was up.

Still, few of the people who came to see this, the finest achievement of British engineering, believed the Tay Bridge was unsafe. Its designer, Thomas Bouch, had built dozens of spans in a career that stretched back three decades, and Queen Victoria herself had been pleased to knight him after crossing the Tay on her way south from Balmoral. The bridge was a triumph that had given the North British company a decisive advantage over its great rival, the Caledonian, in the struggle for the domination of Scotland's railways. It seemed, for eighteen months, that Sir Thomas had conquered the Tay.

But Bouch had been complacent. He had not considered the vicious weather of the Scottish Lowlands. The government inquiry into the disaster, which asked 19 919 questions of 120 witnesses, established that Sir Thomas had made no particular allowance for wind pressure when he designed his slender bridge. He had consulted Sir George Airey, the Astronomer Royal, on the subject and been told it would be sufficient to build a structure capable of withstanding a pressure of 10 pounds per square foot; but on the night of the great storm the wind had been blowing a hurricane, gusting at more than 75 miles per hour and exerting a pressure up to five times greater than the maximum that had been allowed for. On to its fragile girders, with their flawed ironwork, had steamed a train weighing 120 tons. It was just too much for the bridge to bear.

The Tay Bridge disaster created the fiercest of sensations in Victorian Britain. Bouch was disgraced, his design for a still more ambitious bridge across the Firth of Forth was flung aside and he himself died within months of a broken heart. His Tay crossing was eventually replaced, but by a far stronger successor which, while it followed the same curving route across the river and even incorporated thirteen high girders at its centre, was built to cope with the worst the winter weather could throw at it.

The disaster became a defining moment in the history of bridges. More than a century later engineers still hear echoes of the last, awful moments of the flimsy structure as it stood creaking and groaning before the fury of the winter gale, then bent, cracked and crashed down to the icy waters of the river. They are reminded that there are limits to the art of bridge-building more perilous than those governing almost any other branch of engineering, and that each new structure invades a hostile environment as it arches into nothingness and seeks to impose the will of its architect on that of a resistant nature.

Thus, when the designer of any great bridge draws up his plans he has in mind the calamities that have befallen poorly conceived spans, and the lessons to be learned from their destruction.

■ **BRIDGE ACROSS THE GREAT BELT** Sir Thomas Bouch failed to meet the challenge of crossing a shallow if tempestuous river. But bridge-building has progressed far since then. A century later, and hundreds of kilometres to the east, thousands of men went to work on the first bridge to span a sea.

The bridge is Denmark's Storebaelt crossing, the biggest civil engineering project in the country's history and the longest bridge yet built anywhere in the world. When its massive central suspension bridge, currently under construction, has been built it will span the 17.5 kilometre wide Great Belt, the strait that links the Baltic to the North Sea and the Danish mainland to the island of Zealand and the country's capital, Copenhagen.

The Storebaelt project is a multi-billion pound monster designed by consortium and funded by guarantee loans and governments. Companies from Denmark, Britain, Holland, Italy, Germany, Switzerland and the United States have laboured on the bridge while, under their feet, Danes, Frenchmen, Germans and Americans bored a railway tunnel to complement the surface road link. Yet, unusually in a world ruled by computers and committee, one man saw the bridge through the whole of its long struggle for life – an engineer who helped to sketch the original plans, redesigned the spans as technology advanced, and who kept the faith from the moment in 1967 when he first became involved, through the dark years of the 1970s when it appeared the bridge would never be built and he stood almost alone in lobbying for its construction, to the moment when the massive towers of the central pylons began to push skywards by 4 metres a week and the Storebaelt crossing seemed to be a living, growing entity.

Niels Gimsing could hardly be less like Thomas Bouch. Though he favours a deerstalker cap that would not have seemed out of place in Victorian Tayside, he is a thoroughly modern engineer who tempers his enthusiasm for bridges with an academic's precision and a concern for safety alien to the ill-fated Sir Thomas: the structure of the crossing was subjected to lengthy wind tunnel and computer-aided tests designed to ensure it will stand firm in the event of any disaster from a collision to a hurricane.

Such attention to detail was only natural, for Gimsing's challenge was far greater than that facing the builders of the Tay Bridge. While the latter was 3 kilometres long and built on eighty-seven piers, the Storebaelt crossing's central suspension bridge alone will stretch more than half that distance from tower to tower, making it the largest yet constructed anywhere in the world and the first to reach one mile for a single span. It will knock the current record-holder, Britain's Humber Bridge, into second place. Indeed, building the Great Belt link has tested the most modern engineering techniques in every way. The suspension bridge requires the construction of two monolithic concrete pylons to carry its cables, each 254 metres tall – 26 metres higher than those supporting the Golden Gate Bridge in San Francisco. The cables themselves, almost 3 kilometres long, spun from 18 000 wires and the strongest in the world, are close to the limit of what can be done with existing materials.

Almost everything about the project is on the same monumental scale. Travellers from mainland Europe will begin by crossing the Little Belt from Jutland – that long Danish peninsula that reaches up from the German border, bisecting Norway and Sweden to the north – to Funen, the kingdom's second largest island, via a short (1 kilometre) existing bridge. From Funen both cars and trains will head on to an enormous but undramatic low box girder bridge that runs straight out to sea for almost 7 kilometres – this small section of the crossing alone is the second longest bridge in Europe – until it reaches the tiny islet of Sprøgo in the middle of the Great Belt. There the road and rail links will diverge. Trains will enter an 8 kilometre tunnel bored 75 metres below the Baltic sea-bed while cars will continue on to the East Bridge, a somewhat grander box girder design crowned in its centre by the huge suspension bridge.

The irony – yet also the chief glory – of the crossing is the relative ease with which passengers using it will be able to ignore it. A car travelling at motorway speeds should take only 10 minutes to cross from Funen to Zealand and a train a mere seven minutes, cutting by five-sixths the time it took to make the crossing by ferry and turning an awkward journey into an easy drive.

Yet the effect that the completion of the link will have on Denmark can hardly be exaggerated. The Storebaelt crossing will tie what was once of necessity a seafaring nation more closely to Europe, and link a people who have always been divided into East and West Danes; half the population lives on Zealand and half on Jutland and the other scattered islands of the kingdom. 'One of the main reasons for building the bridge,' Gimsing observed, 'is that it unites Denmark. The ferry that runs across the Belt takes time, it's expensive, and it's not really reliable – you have to stop the services under certain weather conditions. And after we joined the European market it became clear that the western part of Denmark has turned more towards the northern part of Germany because they have such easy access to it. Yet I know that when the first bridge across the Little Belt was completed the Danish king felt sad, because he had the feeling that his kingdom was becoming smaller than it had been.'

■ **LONGER, BROADER, STRONGER** The first steps towards bridging the Baltic were taken with the construction of the short span that links Jutland to Funen. The crossing opened in 1935 and was a necessary precursor to any realistic

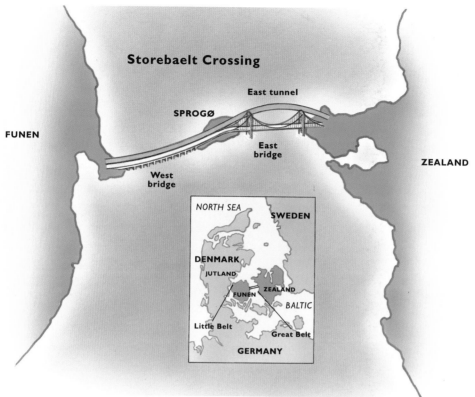

Storebaelt Crossing

East tunnel

SPROGØ

FUNEN

East bridge

West bridge

ZEALAND

NORTH SEA

SWEDEN

DENMARK

JUTLAND

ZEALAND

FUNEN

BALTIC

Little Belt

Great Belt

GERMANY

project for bridging the Great Belt, and its completion inspired practical suggestions for a Jutland–Zealand link. The first plans were drawn up in 1936, the idea was debated in the Danish parliament and, in the spring of 1939, the government authorized soil investigations in the hope of discovering a suitable route for the proposed bridge. But the matter was not pressed with any urgency and the first spadeful of earth had yet to be turned when, in the following year, German troops crossed the border and conquered the country in a day. Even after the war the Danish economy remained depressed and plans for a Great Belt bridge were shelved for a further quarter of a century.

By the 1960s, however, engineers had begun to discuss the idea once again. Learned journals debated rival theories, and in 1965 the government decided to end the search for the best possible bridge by announcing an international contest for designs. The competition was widely publicized and attracted more than a

The Storebaelt crossing will span the Great Belt and link the Danish mainland with the island of Zealand.

A computer simulation of the Storebaelt crossing's central suspension bridge. When it has been completed it will be the longest single span in the world: approximately 1600 metres in length.

hundred entries from as far afield as Australia. Most of the contestants were corporations that had assigned strong teams of experienced engineers and architects the task of drawing up detailed plans; a heavily braced bridge, similar in severity to the massive Forth rail bridge in Scotland, was the option favoured by the majority of the entrants. So there was considerable surprise when the judges announced that the competition had been won not by a multinational consortium but by three Danish engineers, and that the winning design was not a massive truss but an elegant bridge composed of box girders.

The Danes were Niels Gimsing and his friends Jorgen Nissen and Kaj Madsen, and they won because they out-thought their rivals. 'I think we had the only design that presented the idea of splitting the crossing into a road bridge and a railway tunnel,' Gimsing recalled. 'We argued that to split it would give the possibility of lowering the necessary annual investment, because you could start with one link or the other rather than on both simultaneously.'

Even so, it was a startling achievement for three men in their thirties to beat the combined efforts of rivals backed by the resources of major civil engineering firms. In the three decades that have passed since then Gimsing has become a world authority on structural engineering – he acts as a consultant to some of the largest building projects of the century – and, as a full professor at one of Denmark's leading universities, mentor to a whole new generation of Danish engineers.

Niels Gimsing loves bridges. He may be a practical man, capable of sizing up a structure at a glance, calculating why it stands and what it would take to knock it down; but he is also a connoisseur who appreciates the beauty of a design and applauds bridges built with consideration for their surroundings. 'Absolute priority,' he explained, 'is given to building a safe bridge, and then to fulfilling the require- ments of traffic. After that, though, the next priority should be aesthetics. That is because large bridges are very dominating. The Great Belt bridge will be by far the largest structure built in Denmark in the twentieth century, so it would be very wrong to make it ugly.'

Though the competition was won in 1967, plans to bridge the Belt foun- dered in a maelstrom of political

The principal engineer of Denmark's record- breaking Storebaelt bridge, Niels Gimsing, has spent a quarter of a century labouring on his masterpiece: He and his two colleagues won the competition to design the crossing in 1967.

debates, environmental wrangles, redesigns and official apathy – enough to have discouraged all but the most visionary, or stubborn, men. Not until 1976 did the Danish parliament authorize the creation of a bridge authority to oversee detailed design work on a Great Belt link. Niels Gimsing was hired to help with this work, but within two years the government hit financial problems. The national debt was rising sharply, and there was not enough money to build the bridge and also develop a distribution network for the North Sea gas that everyone had been told would save the country. The shutters clattered down at the Great Belt bridge authority, and they stayed down for five long years.

The earlier delays had been frustrating, but this time Gimsing was sure the bridge really had been wished away. 'They called it a postponement, but I had a strong feeling they just didn't dare announce that the bridge would never be built. I was very upset – I really believed that the link would not happen in my lifetime,' he recalled. So he began to agitate. He wrote a book to promote the idea of the bridge and prove it could be affordable and made safe for navigation. He talked to politicians and to journalists. And he persuaded them. In 1983 yet another committee was formed to examine the prospects for a fixed link, and Niels Gimsing was named its chairman.

The design of the bridge had to take account of prevailing conditions in the Baltic. Fortunately the Great Belt is a relatively shallow stretch of water, so siting the dozens of enormous concrete caissons – watertight chambers – on which the bridge would be built presented no great problems. Nor is there a threat from earthquakes. But the Storebaelt crossing had to be strong enough to withstand collisions and designed to ensure that traffic on the bridge would be safe even in winter weather. The lessons of the Tay disaster had been learned, and everyone agreed the crossing might have to be closed for an hour or two each year in particularly bad weather. But the prevailing winds blow parallel to, rather than across, the bridge and there were contingency plans to erect perforated windshields on the elevated section between Sprøgo and Zealand.

Far more time and effort had to be devoted to the environmental stipulations that became the main concern of the Danish government. As the first bridge ever to span the approaches to an entire sea, the Storebaelt crossing was closely scrutinized to ensure that its construction did not upset the ecology of the area or the flow of water between the North Sea and the Baltic. About 70 per cent of the water entering and leaving the Baltic passes through the Great Belt, and it was calculated that the construction of the massive caissons would cut the flow by no more than a third of one per cent. However, the government insisted that there be no alteration overall – the so-called 'zero solution' – and the companies building the bridge have had to dredge almost 37 million tons of mud and sand from the sea-bed to keep the flow of water unchanged.

A number of studies have suggested that building the bridge will have little long-term impact on the animal populations of the Belt – chiefly herring, mussels and eider ducks. But the need to dispose of the dredged soil, and financial considerations that dictate that it is far cheaper to build bridges on land than in water, had one major environmental effect. The construction of the crossing meant the destruction of the calm and peaceful islet of Sprøgo and its replacement with a largely artificial island, created from the dredged soil, that is four times the size of the old one and half-covered by the bridge, the railway tunnel and their approaches.

The decision to remodel Sprøgo was taken to minimize the environmental impact of the bridge on the Great Belt as a whole. The alternative would have been to build an artificial island slightly to the north, a more expensive option that would have required additional compensatory dredging and still spoilt the peace and quiet that made the island special.

Furthermore, taking the route of the crossing well away from Sprøgo would have meant moving into wider and deeper waters and also extending existing road and rail links on Funen and Zealand. This would have doubled the cost of the project, already budgeted at more than 20 billion Danish kroner (around £2.2 billion). As it is, Denmark's motorists and railway passengers will be paying for the Storebaelt crossing in the form of tolls and ticket prices well into the twenty-first century. With the payback period fixed by a decision to peg tolls to the cost of ferry tickets, the bridge should finally move into the black in 2013.

■ **THE ARCH, THE GIRDER AND THE CABLE-STAYED** The secrets of a bridge's design are to be found not in its girders and trusses, its pylons or its towers, but in the empty space below. The more severe the terrain it has to cross, the fewer options remain open to its designers. Mundane obstacles make for boring and formulaic spans – over motorways, for example – but terrible difficulties have inspired engineers to create great bridges.

The Storebaelt crossing will be a fine example of this general rule. In several respects the Great Belt poses few real challenges to the bridge-builder; its water is relatively shallow, the current placid and the tides unspectacular. But the Belt is a great shipping channel, and the need to build a bridge big enough to ensure safe navigation beneath it caused seemingly endless delays and headaches for designers.

The original design for the crossing bears little resemblance to the bridge that will eventually be built across the Belt and seems modest compared to the complex plans that were eventually implemented. It called for a bridge that was long, certainly, but also relatively simple and based on the box girder principle used almost a century earlier in the building of the Tay Bridge.

The needs of shipping, as they stood in the late 1960s, had been catered for by a clause in the original competition rules specifying that a central span of at least 350 metres be left to allow safe navigation. However, even then Gimsing and his colleagues had suspected that this clearance would not be enough, and their entry opted for caution by allowing for twin 400 metre spans at the centre of the bridge: one for ships travelling north, the other for vessels sailing south. The decision involved some complex work. A 400 metre girder was huge – one and a half times longer than any that had been built before – and it was vital to discover whether their proposal exceeded the limits of what was possible. They had to investigate the properties of new high-strength steels before concluding that their design was sound.

Their prize-winning plan was probably safe for ships navigating the Great Belt at the time, but as the size of the vessels passing through the strait rose during the 1970s and 1980s and a channel once chiefly the preserve of steamers and fishing boats became busy with tankers and bulk carriers, the bridge's design was modified not once but several times. While the box girder approaches remained largely unchanged, the central span grew to incorporate 600 metres of clearance between its central pylons, and then 780 metres.

Most engineers were confident that with more than three-quarters of a kilometre of sea-room to manoeuvre in, even large vessels would be able to pass under the bridge in perfect safety. But when designs for the crossing were being finalized in 1988, Gimsing recommended that the engineers take advantage of one of Denmark's newest resources to conduct definitive final tests. He turned to the programmers at the Danish Maritime Institute's Marine Simulation System, a high-tech computer simulator that tests the performance of vessels in a wide variety of imaginary scenarios. Although the system is built around powerful banks of computers, it is operated by seamen who stand on a replica of a ship's bridge, complete with engine telegraph, radar and wheel, while computer screens show the view fore and aft, to port and starboard. The DMI system, which is normally used to train mariners in the safest way to enter harbour, was reprogrammed to simulate the waterway beneath a variety of designs for bridges over the Great Belt. When all the variables of current, wind and weather were stored in the program's memory, expert navigators were assigned the task of guiding their imaginary ships beneath the central span under different conditions. The final trial involved two large ships passing each other beneath the bridge.

Each possible scenario was carefully tested and the results came as a surprise to those who had believed that their design made generous allowance for shipping. 'All the crews agreed that 780 metres would be absolutely unacceptable,' Gimsing recalled. 'The risks of colliding either with the bridge or with another ship moving in the opposite direction were very evident. So we decided to test a larger range of bridges, and discovered that you would have to produce a span of approximately 1600 metres.'

The gradual evolution of the Storebaelt bridge from a long but relatively simple design to one that incorporates the longest single span yet built, meant that Gimsing had to deploy his detailed knowledge of the history of bridge-building and of the relative merits of the half-dozen or so principal ways of engineering a crossing. This store of experience enabled him to borrow techniques developed by his many great predecessors and to learn from the problems they struggled to overcome.

The girder bridge to which Gimsing originally turned was a solution born of the Industrial Revolution. Before its invention practically all bridges were built of stone or metal arches, using designs perfected by the Romans in the construction of many spectacularly long-lived structures. Surviving Roman bridges include the Ponte Sant'Angelo – still standing and still carrying traffic over the Tiber into the centre of Rome almost 2000 years after its completion – and the dramatic, three-tiered Pont du Gard, near Nimes, which took troops and water over a deep gorge and which survives in close to its original form despite having been built almost entirely without the use of mortar. All of them testify to the strength of a well-constructed arch. The principle is simple; the load borne by the bridge is directed out and down on to solid foundations, while the stones that form the arch itself are compressed, adding stability and minimizing any risk of collapse.

Arched bridges provided a solution to many of the construction problems of the ancient world and are still popular today. But they have two great limitations. As the span of an arch increases, its height must rise if it is to retain its strength; even a relatively shallow arch 1600 metres wide would have to be almost half a kilometre high – massive enough to put it, if not literally up in the clouds, at least out of the reach of the Danish government's pocket. And one high enough to allow the largest vessel to pass beneath its centre still offers only a relatively narrow navigation channel. A tall ship risks colliding with its sloping walls as they curve down to sea-level.

It was the latter difficulty that inspired Robert Stephenson, son of the great railway engineer, to stretch the limits of existing metal spans when he designed the Britannia railway bridge over the Menai Strait to Anglesey, a mile to the south of Thomas Telford's more famous suspension bridge. Design work was bedevilled by a protracted dispute with the Royal Navy, which successfully prevented the construction of an arch on the grounds that it would close part of the channel to shipping. The width of the strait at the chosen point was judged too great for a suspension bridge, so Stephenson was forced to turn to girders. Construction began in the late 1840s.

By this time there was nothing new about metal bridges – the first, the famous Ironbridge at Coalbrookdale in Staffordshire, had been completed in 1779 – but the width of the spans required by Stephenson's design made a simple girder bridge impracticable. A girder rests on pylons at either side but is unsupported in its centre, and its limits are determined by the strength and stiffness of the material it is made from; iron girders strong enough to support the trains envisaged by Stephenson would have to be so deep and so massive that simply lifting them into place, more than 230 feet above the strait, would have proved impossible. The

Roman engineers built the Pont du Gard almost entirely without the use of mortar. It combined roadways with an aqueduct.

solution was to forge hollow wrought-iron structures. These new girders, strong but light, were the result of careful experiments carried out for Stephenson by the great Scottish shipbuilder Sir William Fairbairn. He demonstrated the superior compressive strength of straight rather than curved sheets of iron, and advised Stephenson to build his bridge from rectangular rather than circular girders; his experiments had shown that only sharp-angled girders would be strong enough to support a train in the centre of the bridge without buckling.

Even today, the designs for the girder sections of the Storebaelt crossing owe a debt to Stephenson's work. The long, low West Bridge, which connects Funen to Sprøgo, is made up of six huge expansion sections, each more than a kilometre long and comprising two separate box girders, one to carry road traffic and the other rail. The box girders are cast in sections of 18 metres and 27 metres and five sections are joined to make one girder. These spans are supported on pillars that rise 18 metres above the sea, enough to allow small vessels to pass underneath the bridge, and are designed to bear not only their own weight and that of the traffic crossing them, but also substantial extra loads in the form of the ice that forms in the Great Belt every ten years or so.

However, as Gimsing discovered when it became apparent that the 400 metre spans in the original designs for the Storebaelt crossing did not allow sufficient clearance for shipping, even box girder bridges exhibit weaknesses when their spans exceed around 500 metres. Long girder bridges are possible only where numerous

piers can be built to support them; deep gorges and channels can pose insuperable problems, and here engineers turn to alternative designs such as the cantilever bridge that require fewer pylons.

Perhaps the most famous cantilever structure – and Gimsing's favourite bridge – is the Firth of Forth rail crossing which spans the deep waters of the inlet at the very spot where Sir Thomas Bouch would have built his bridge had his theories not been proved fatally flawed by

The West Bridge runs for 6.6 kilometres from Funen to the islet of Sprøgo and is itself the second longest bridge in Europe.

the disaster on the Tay. It was built soon after the collapse of the Tay crossing and it is not surprising that the North British company chose a massively reinforced bridge in which load-bearing girders were strongly braced above and below by trusses made of heavy metal tubes. Its designers were far better qualified than Bouch: John Fowler, the youngest ever president of the Institution of Civil Engineers and Benjamin Baker, who had already proved himself an engineer of rare talent. Fowler and Baker took full advantage of their new freedom to build in steel, which had only just been legalized for use in bridges, and designed what was surely the strongest bridge of its era. It was opened in 1889, in the midst of a gale, but Baker had insisted that his structure be capable of withstanding wind pressures of up to 56 pounds per square foot, and those crossing the bridge felt not the slightest hint of danger.

The great depth of the firth had prevented the construction of pylons in the water, and though Baker and his colleague considered several suspension designs the need for strength dictated a span based on girders. Their solution, the distinctive cantilever bridge that still stands today, depended on the construction of a central pier on the one suitable spot in the river: Inchgarvie Island. A pier had, indeed, already been built there to link the slender dual suspension bridges decided on by Sir Thomas Bouch, but Baker's was made far stronger in order to support the girders that stretch out from the island and from either bank towards two central cantilever spans which are supported by trusses.

The cantilever principle can be seen as an interim solution to a problem now generally solved with a suspension bridge. Its central spans, which Baker demonstrated could be adequately supported by transferring the load from the suspended girders to his massive piers, allowed the construction of a bridge longer than would have been possible with a box girder design; only late in the twentieth century have advances in materials and techniques allowed the construction of suspension bridges of similar strength.

What attracted Gimsing to the Forth rail crossing, aside from its awe-inspiring if hardly beautiful design, was the way in which it boldly smashed existing Victorian records for bridge design. Although a much smaller cantilever span had previously been built in Germany, it was the first major British structure to utilize the principle and was three times longer than any railway crossing built before the Tay Bridge. With a total length of $2\frac{1}{2}$ kilometres, it was in any case almost as long as Bouch's span over the Tay; and it was taller and used more steel (55 000 tons, including the weight of its $6\frac{1}{2}$ million rivets) than any rival.

'It requires a very brave man to go beyond the limits that have been set before that time,' Gimsing said, 'and of course the further you go the braver you have to be. With the background of the Tay Bridge disaster it was very impressive to take such a big step. The bridge was very extraordinary at the time it was built – much larger than any other. The concept and even the structural material was new, and the geometry of the trusses is so complex it would be difficult to calculate even with the computers we have today. Because the suspension bridge became favoured for long-span bridges it is also still the largest truss bridge anywhere in the world.'

Indeed, massive designs of the Forth type are now quite out of favour among bridge-builders. Aside from their expense – they use more steel than any comparable form of span – they are awkward and costly to maintain. The job of painting the Forth Bridge is, famously, a never-ending one. The introduction of modern forms of steel that are between two and three times as strong as the best available to Baker and Fowler has effectively made the truss redundant.

As the width required of the Storebaelt crossing's central span increased, a cheaper and more modern type of bridge came under consideration. This was the cable-stayed design, a relative of the suspension bridge, that had been perfected

The deep water of the Forth estuary prevented Benjamin Baker, one of the principal engineers employed on its crossing, from building his bridge on a number of pylons. Limited to a massive pier on Inchgarvie Island, he settled on a cantilever design, using two stayed pylons to support a central span, and illustrated the basic principle with this 'living model'.

only in the 1950s. A stayed bridge supports its load-bearing girders directly with cables that run up to massive pylons of the suspension bridge type. Such bridges are relatively simple to build; once the pylons are constructed, workmen begin to move out simultaneously from both sides towards the middle, adding supporting cables as they go. One advantage is that materials and pre-fabricated sections can be brought along the constructed portion of the bridge to where they are needed, without the necessity for the heavy lifting that can cause problems in building a suspension bridge. On the other hand, engineers have to be careful to allow for the problem of immense half-spans swaying laterally in the wind as they move out into the void. This sort of motion makes it extremely difficult to join the two sides of the bridge when they finally meet. Until very recently it was thought to limit the cable-stayed design to a span of around half a kilometre – that is, a maximum of 250 metres on either side before the two sections meet.

Today that limit has been exceeded in France, where the ambitious Pont du Normandie, across the mouth of the Seine near Le Havre, has been completed. Its central span is 856 metres across, almost half as long again as the previous record-holder in China, and is held in place by dozens of cables radiating from towers more than 200 metres tall. But beating that record caused many headaches for the French engineers. They had to abandon their original plan to anchor the part-completed span to the river banks with cables when local sailors protested at the potential danger to shipping, and substitute a system of 50 ton counterweights designed to counteract the oscillations caused by high winds.

A bridge the size of the Pont du Normandie would have been just large enough to span the central section of the Storebaelt crossing – until the 1989 experiments with Denmark's Marine Simulation System proved the need for at least 1600 metres of clearance to allow safe navigation through the Belt. This further substantial increase in specifications left the Danes with only one real alternative: the Storebaelt project would have to be crowned with a gigantic suspension bridge.

Suspension bridges, the most graceful and beautiful of spans, are often thought of as modern – some of the most famous recent designs, including Britain's successful Severn and Humber crossings, are built this way. At the very least, most people who use them suppose they are inventions of the industrial age that date back little further than the days when Isambard Kingdom Brunel was sketching

The Forth rail bridge was British engineering's response to the Tay Bridge disaster. 55 000 tons of steel were used in its construction and 6½ million rivets were hammered in. It was opened in a storm and has stood firm ever since.

ideas for the Clifton Suspension Bridge at Bristol. On the contrary, the idea of supporting a crossing by hanging it from ropes or chains or cables goes back beyond the dawn of history. Rope suspension bridges were made in Asia and in South America and the Chinese were early masters of the art.

The enormous flexibility of the suspension bridge principle makes it today the most popular choice for any span crossing a chasm or deep water. Although it is neither the simplest nor the cheapest type of structure to build, it is strong and has the great advantage, compared to cable-stayed bridges, that the cables which support the main deck are hung first and the deck sections are then pre-fabricated and hoisted into place so that there is always adequate support while it is being built.

When planning a suspension bridge, therefore, a designer starts by calculating the weight of his main deck because this will determine the strength of the cables needed to support it; but he will be limited by the maximum load a modern cable can bear. In the case of the Storebaelt crossing, calculations revealed that the cables needed to be no less than 800 millimetres thick and they were spun *in situ* by machines weaving thousands and thousands of 5 millimetre wires.

The next stage is extensive wind tunnel testing, which shows whether the structure will be stable in high winds. Such experiments are important because suspension bridges are relatively flimsy and there has been at least one modern instance in which poor design led to the disastrous collapse of the central span.

The incident occurred in Washington State, where in the late 1930s the engineer Leon Moissieff built an exceptionally slender suspension bridge over the Tacoma Narrows of Puget Sound. During construction, it was noticed that workers who went out on to the structure often developed motion sickness caused by the deck's movement in the wind, and when the bridge, which had a span of just over 850 metres (2800 feet), opened in July 1940 it soon attracted hundreds of sightseers who enjoyed the thrill of crossing the pitching central section as it rippled and writhed beneath them in the lightest of winds. Attempts to dampen the motion by adding additional cable stays to the deck helped to limit the problem. But in the autumn of the first year these stabilizing cables snapped and it was immediately apparent that the bridge's swaying motion had changed for the worse. Where once the central span had merely lurched up and down, it now began to yaw. Only four months after its grand opening the bridge, nicknamed 'Galloping Gertie', was caught in a steady wind of around 68 kilometres per hour which caused it to twist, buckle and finally crash into the waters of the sound. Fortunately, no one was injured in the disaster, but a newsreel cameraman who was on the scene captured the bridge's spectacular death throes in a film now routinely shown to new generations of engineers as a visual warning of the dangers of poor design.

Helped by the evidence of the film, investigators were able to discover the cause of the collapse. It stemmed from the deck design. Leon Mossieff had replaced the traditional criss-crossing struts of a truss with a slender girder with a flat, square side. When wind hit the sharp edge of the deck, it formed tiny whirlwinds that started it twisting.

Twisting bridges are incredibly dangerous – with each twist, more of the deck is turned towards the wind so that it twists even more until it tears itself apart. Engineers' immediate reaction to the disaster was to return to the old deck design – the heavy ironwork of the traditional truss – which breaks up the wind as it hits the bridge and saves the structure from the twisting torments of miniature whirlwinds.

It was the 1960s before engineers reconsidered the fundamental problem of wind pressure and came up with a solution. The breakthrough was the work of Fritz Leonhardt, Gimsing's predecessor as doyen of European bridge designers. His theory was that by careful testing it should be possible to produce a suspension bridge whose deck was shaped, like a wing, to minimize air resistance and prevent the setting up of dangerous whirlwinds and oscillations. His revolutionary designs were safe, slender and, by saving on materials, relatively cheap to build.

Unlike cable-stay spans, which can look hard and ugly, suspension bridges have an enviable grace. 'It's almost impossible to make a suspension bridge look bad,' Gimsing said. 'The whole appearance of the bridge is governed by slender cables and there is something majestic about them – the towers are taller than the towers on the large cathedrals that were built in previous centuries.'

Attractive lines are certainly evident in the road bridge, opened in 1966, that crosses the river Severn on the border between England and Wales. It and its younger sister, the Humber crossing (a span very much from the same school of design), have influenced most subsequent major European suspension bridges, including the one in Istanbul that links Europe to Asia across the Bosporus.

Gimsing too benefited from the experience of the British designers who built the Severn and Humber bridges, and he was pleased by the beauty of the finished design – slender yet strong – for Denmark's great suspension bridge. The deck, like that of the Humber Bridge, is formed from a closed box, which makes maintenance easy, and is designed as an aerofoil so that wind will flow over and under it rather than battering its sides and forming dangerous vortices. Exhaustive tunnel tests have shown that the bridge will be stable at wind speeds of up to 72 metres per second – more than twice what has ever been recorded in the vicinity of the Great Belt.

The Danes are determined there shall be no repeat of the Tay Bridge disaster in the waters of the Baltic.

■ **LONGER: THE ERA OF THE SUPER-BRIDGE** The completion of the Storebaelt crossing will usher in a new age of super-bridges that are longer, taller and more complex than any that came before them. Like it, they will cross seas rather than rivers. And where earlier spans linked communities and changed countries, these new designs will link countries and change continents.

Plans are already well advanced for the completion of the first fixed link between northern Europe and Scandinavia, of which the Storebaelt crossing forms the major part. To the spans that run from Jutland to Funen, from Funen to Sprøgo, and from Sprøgo to Zealand, will be added a bridge and a tunnel across the Øresund, the narrow channel that separates Denmark from Sweden. It will be 7.5 kilometres long and, fittingly, Niels Gimsing, Jorgen Nissen and Kaj Madsen are working together on its design.

In many respects it is less ambitious than the Storebaelt Bridge. The waters of the Øresund are extremely shallow, making the construction of foundations for the

The collapse of the Tacoma Narrows suspension bridge in Washington State provided a graphic illustration of the dangers of underestimating the power of the wind. These photographs show how 'Galloping Gertie' swayed in the wind before breaking up. Film of the disaster is still shown, as a warning, to new generations of bridge engineers.

pylons relatively easy, and the existing navigation channel is a mere 300 metres wide. Because of this the crossing – a twin-level truss design carrying cars on its upper deck and trains below – will be crowned by a cable-stayed bridge with a span of only 490 metres (which will, nevertheless, be the longest in the world to carry both a motorway and a railway). However, there are new difficulties. The structure will be longer than either the east or west portions of the Storebaelt crossing and, because it will be built close to Copenhagen, it will be relatively expensive – the cost of buying land for the approach roads has pushed the price to two-thirds that of the Great Belt link. Worse, the proximity of the city's airport has made it impossible to build a bridge direct from Denmark to Sweden as the structure could be a hazard to aircraft. Instead, the crossing will begin with a road and rail tunnel that leads out under the Øresund and emerges 4 kilometres out to sea on an artificial island built from tunnel spoil. Only then will traffic drive on to a bridge that arches the remaining 7.5 kilometres east. But both the Danish and the Swedish governments are convinced that these are problems worth overcoming. When the Storebaelt and the Øresund links are open it will be possible to drive the 250 kilometres from Germany to Sweden in just two and a half hours – a journey that today takes more than six hours and is interrupted by two ferry crossings.

Although the Storebaelt link will be the world's longest bridge and its suspension bridge is its longest single span, the record will soon be snatched by the Japanese. Work is already well advanced on the Honshu–Shikoku Bridge project, a scheme to link two of the four large islands that make up Japan via three separate crossings. The first, a meandering succession of truss, suspension and cable-stayed structures, is already complete; in all, these bridges and their linking viaducts run for around 10 kilometres and cross half a dozen islets. Each has two decks, one for rail traffic and the other for road traffic, and together they make up the largest civil engineering project in history. Meanwhile, construction work continues on the other two, still more ambitious, spans. One is an 890 metre cable-stayed design that will be the longest bridge of its kind when it is finished in 1999 (exceeding the limit set by the Pont du Normandie by just 34 metres), and which lies at the centre of a 60 kilometre link running across an archipelago. The other, the Akashi Kaikyo, will be the suspension bridge that beats the Storebaelt span into second place.

The Akashi Kaikyo Bridge, scheduled for completion in 1998, will have a span

The record for the world's longest single span will return to Europe from Japan if current plans for a giant suspension bridge across the Strait of Messina are given the go-ahead. The project has been thoroughly researched but still awaits funding. The central span will be 3.3 kilometres in length and the finished bridge promises to dwarf its surroundings.

of 1990 metres and towers an awe-inspiring 297 metres high. Like the Storebaelt link, it has been designed to cross one of the world's busiest waterways, but in many respects it has tested the ingenuity of its designers to an even greater extent than Gimsing and his colleagues were tested. The Akashi Strait is much deeper than the Great Belt so 70 metre deep piers are needed; currents are strong and the threat from earthquakes is very real. The structure, designed to withstand the shock of a quake 150 kilometres away that measures 8.5 on the Richter scale, was damaged by the Kobe earthquake in January 1995 and one of its anchor blocks was displaced by 1.5 metres.

The Akashi Kaikyo is a stupendous achievement by any standards, but if European bridge designers have their way the Japanese ascendancy will be short-lived. Gimsing himself is involved in the early stages of an attempt to build what is by far the most ambitious suspension bridge yet conceived: a gigantic project that will link Sicily to the Italian mainland over the Strait of Messina.

If it is built the crossing will have a central span an astonishing 3.3 kilometres in length, far outstripping its Japanese rival. What is even more impressive, it will be supported by cables strung from towers that soar 376 metres above the waters of the Mediterranean, dwarfing local buildings and even the hills at the toe of Italy. Like the Akashi Kaikyo Bridge, the whole edifice will have to be earthquake resistant, while the Strait of Messina is so deep – 120 metres and more – that several studies sponsored by the Italian government concluded that it would be impracticable to sink any pylons in the sea itself. The towers will have to be sited at the edge of the strait itself.

'The location would make it a very beautiful structure,' an admiring Gimsing remarked. 'You have mountains on either side of the strait, and the bridge crossing the entire width. I think it could compete with the Golden Gate Bridge, and having a span two and a half times that of the Golden Gate would in itself be very impressive.'

To allow the Messina Strait Bridge to carry the planned twin railway tracks and three-carriage motorways, plus service and emergency lanes, the east and west carriageways will have to be separated not by solid steel or concrete, but by lightweight grids that will supply the required strength at only a fraction of the weight. Even so, the huge span will be so long that Gimsing has calculated that almost half of the massive suspension cables' strength will be taken up simply in supporting their own weight. These hawsers will be right at the limit of suspension bridge design. To build a suspension bridge significantly longer than Messina's will involve more than ordering more concrete and steel. It will require the creation of whole new families of composites and alloys, and the development of revolutionary ways of deploying them.

Few engineers doubt that this will happen, and that spans of 4, 5 or maybe even 10 kilometres will eventually be built. Such structures could form part of the still bigger bridges that have been suggested. It is theoretically possible to link Spain to Morocco across another major shipping lane, the 19 kilometre Strait of Gibraltar. And an American designer has even suggested bridging the last great channel between continents – the 80 kilometre Bering Strait between the Arctic territories of Russia and the United States – with a link comprising dozens of short spans.

The construction of such super-bridges will depend, of course, as much on financial necessity and political willpower as it will on engineering prowess, but if any of these ambitious plans ever gets the go-ahead, it will test again the limits of the bridge-builder's skill. For Gimsing though, even the chance to work on one of these spectacular projects is unlikely to prove more satisfying than witnessing the final completion of the Storebaelt crossing, the bridge that has been part of his life for more than a quarter of a century.

CHAPTER TWO

DEEP

The Institution of Civil Engineers looms over Great George Street, opposite the Houses of Parliament in the heart of London. Built solidly of stone during the reign of Victoria, it lived through the Blitz. But in the 1990s this great grey monument faced a new danger – not a bomb whistling from the sky but a metal worm creeping towards it underground, twisting and turning through the city's maze of subterranean obstacles to pass only metres below its foundations. If the worm had come just a fraction too close, the foundations would have shifted and those solid walls would have cracked and split, causing more than just embarrassment for the man who set it on its way: Hugh Doherty, tunneller, himself one of the Institution's most distinguished members.

Doherty's 'worm' is an enormous tunnelling machine that is excavating the biggest addition to the London underground railway network for a quarter of a century. The Jubilee Line Extension is designed to run from Green Park station in Piccadilly down to Westminster, past Big Ben and the Houses of Parliament, then under the Thames and County Hall to link Waterloo, London Bridge and Bermondsey to the Docklands and Canary Wharf in the east and provide the first east-west underground line south of the river. Leaving the Isle of Dogs it will burrow under the river and emerge in the derelict, abandoned North Greenwich peninsula – now chosen as the site of an urban renewal programme crowned by the largest underground station in Europe. From there the tunnel will turn through 90 degrees to emerge north of the Thames as an overground railway terminating in Stratford. All in all, the £2 billion scheme calls for the construction of a line that stretches for 16 kilometres, and runs for three-quarters of its length through new tunnels excavated to the tightest of tight deadlines through dangerously unstable terrain.

The millions of Londoners who use the Underground each year to get to work or travel around the capital tend to take the network for granted. But for Doherty the Jubilee Line Extension, or JLE, is a challenge so phenomenal, so studded with difficulty, that when he undertook the project he understood immediately that its completion would be the pinnacle of his career. 'At Westminster,' he explained, 'we have to tunnel under all the famous buildings without damaging them. At London Bridge we are using a tunnelling method never used before in central London. And

**Previous page:
Parts of the Jubilee
Line Extension are
being excavated by
the New Austrian
Tunnelling Method.**

down in the East End we have to tunnel under the river in some of the most treacherous ground imaginable – so treacherous nobody has tried to build a tunnel there for over a hundred years. The JLE is the big one – more complex than the Channel Tunnel. It is the challenge of a lifetime; everything after it will be an anticlimax for me.'

Doherty is not exaggerating. The Jubilee Line Extension is one of the biggest infrastructure schemes in Europe, so big that the only way of completing it within the specified fifty-three months was to split the work into twelve major contracts, awarded to some of the most famous names in civil engineering. The whole gigantic project – thirty-six major sites and eleven new stations – has to be built to remarkably tight deadlines, and there are punitive fines for any company that fails to complete work on time.

Doherty has under his control tunnellers working for British, Japanese, French and Austrian companies, many of which are in joint ventures and all of which are responsible to one of his two principal lieutenants: Joe Stacey, a former Channel Tunnel and Hong Kong mass transit man, as construction manager west; and Terry Kirkpatrick, for thirty years an officer of the Royal Engineers, as construction manager east. The largest contract, 102, was awarded jointly to the civil engineering groups Balfour Beatty and AMEC, is valued at £157 million and calls for the two companies to bore twin 2.5 kilometre long tunnels under the Thames between Green Park and Waterloo and build Jubilee Line stations at Westminster and Waterloo. The joint venture was given only 200 weeks to complete possibly the most complex contract on the project.

The tight, interlocking schedules mean that one of the team's biggest worries is constantly balancing speed against quality. On the one hand it is imperative to keep each contract on time and to focus all the project team's attention on getting any that fall behind back on course; on the other, the work has to be built to last. The contracts issued by London Underground call for the tunnels and stations built for the extension to have a life of at least 120 years. The excellent condition of the existing network – much of it dug in the nineteenth century – suggests it is not too much to hope that the tunnels will still be in use in the year 2400.

'It's important,' Doherty explained, 'to get the project delivered on time and to budget. But if you focus on the time element then that will generally help you with the budget element. If you get the time wrong, your budget will be wrong – so the main focus is on time, and that in itself will help to take care of the budget.'

Speed and safety in tunnelling are invariably dependent on one thing: soil conditions. In hard ground, matters are relatively simple. Tunnelling through rock means using explosives to blast a way through – a dangerous business, certainly, but relatively quick because most such tunnels are self-supporting. Many experienced tunnellers consider that the ideal ground is chalk marl, which is soft enough to be excavated by machine, yet sufficiently firm to make the danger of a cave-in remote. The Channel Tunnel was dug through chalk; because of this, engineers always regarded it as a logistical challenge rather than an engineering nightmare.

It is different in the soft soils under London. Although it is easier to bore through earth than rock, each tunnel must be laboriously propped and secured against the dangers of a cave-in. The world record for excavating something the size of a Jubilee Line tunnel is 501 metres driven in five days – a record achieved during the construction of London's water ring main in the late 1980s. The conditions facing the men on the JLE are rarely so favourable, and in the east only the latest technology makes the waterlogged soil around the Thames passable at all.

'It is a notorious industry,' Doherty conceded. 'The men are brave, and they have to be, basically because of soil conditions. It doesn't matter how many times you survey the soil along the route, you could still come across unknown soil, find yourself using the wrong machine for the wrong soil – and then you've got a problem.'

A glance at the top-heavy London Underground map with its lines and hundreds of its stations concentrated on the north bank of the Thames underlines the difficulty of tunnelling south of the river. Although the network has more than twenty stations there, most of the lines that service them run above ground. There is a simple reason for this. North of the Thames, most of the city is built on a solid bed of what is known as London Clay, a stiff, grey-brown soil made of extremely fine particles originally deposited on what was, millions of years ago, the bed of a deep, calm sea. London Clay is a fine material for tunnelling. It is cohesive and reasonably self-supporting, so the dangers of a cave-in are low, and its regular consistency means that tunnellers can dig at speed without worrying about the risks of striking dangerous ground ahead.

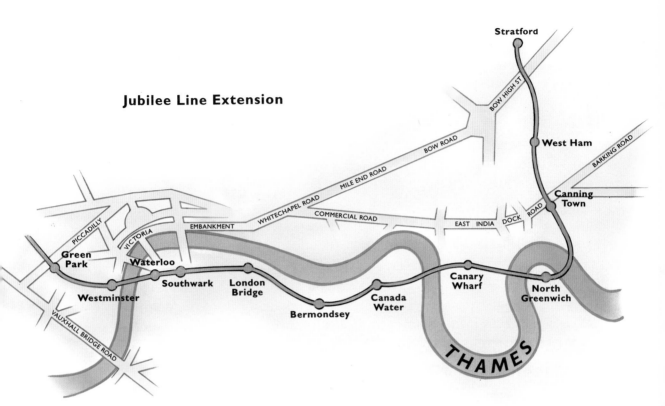

Jubilee Line Extension

To the south and east, on the other hand, deeper strata of water-bearing sand and gravel known to geologists as the Woolwich and Reading Beds come to the surface. They can be so saturated that they become semi-liquid and threaten to cascade into a working. Water lying in them can also be quite highly pressurized so that engineers are forced to pressurize their workfaces to prevent sudden inrushes. Underneath runs an especially unpleasant layer of quicksand called the Thanet Sands, deposited there in less settled geological times. 'Terrible stuff,' according to Doherty. 'It doesn't stand up; as soon as you tunnel into it it collapses. And it doesn't hold water at all, so when you're tunnelling the water rushes out of it.'

Thus, while plans for an underground line south of the river have been mooted for years, it is only relatively recently that tunnelling technology has advanced to the point where a link is both practicable and economical.

The Jubilee Line Extension will cross the Thames four times on its way from Green Park in London's West End to Stratford in the east. Its route goes through some of the most treacherous conditions tunnel engineers have ever had to face.

In several important respects, therefore, the Jubilee Line Extension is unlike most of the tunnelling work that has been carried out on the London Underground in the last century. It is unusual in that it will link new areas of the city to the network, rather than seeking to relieve congestion in the centre of the capital. It is also the first underground line to be funded partly by private capital. This is vital to the project and has helped to determine its course. The JLE has its roots in a proposed £400 million direct link from Waterloo to Docklands which was intended to ferry office workers to the developments around Canary Wharf. When London Underground ruled that this was too specific to meet east London's public transport needs, the developers offered to switch their funding to the Jubilee Line project so long as the underground link ran through the Isle of Dogs; and when the recession forced them into administration the start date for the main tunnelling work was put back for two years while lengthy negotiations proceeded with the receivers.

This delay, while immensely frustrating, did give Doherty's project team the opportunity to re-examine some of the advance work for the new line. More than £3 million had already been spent on comprehensively investigating the ground through which the tunnels would be driven in order to minimize the risk of striking unexpected hazards. Boreholes were drilled through all the surface strata until an underlying layer of chalk was struck, and solid cores of soil were extracted by the hundred. A number of trial pits were also dug; fortunately, the results showed that ground conditions for the project were broadly favourable. To the west, in the most congested area, London Clay would at least make it possible for Doherty's men to excavate the caverns needed for new stations and ticket halls underneath existing structures; to the east, where unfavourable ground would make such large scale work hazardous, the line passes through many semi-derelict zones of depressed inner city where it would generally be possible to dig down from the surface using London Underground's traditional 'open box' method of building – a 'cut and cover' technique that calls for the excavation of a gigantic pit in which a new station can be built from the floor up, then roofed over and covered with the spoil.

Hugh Doherty, the engineer in overall charge of the Jubilee Line Extension project, is charged with keeping work at thirty-six separate sites on schedule. He learned his trade on the dangerous Clyde Tunnel project in the 1960s.

Little else about the Jubilee Line Extension is traditional. It is a new sort of underground railway, a deliberate attempt to get away from the claustrophobic platforms and baffling labyrinth of foot tunnels that make up the existing network north of the river. The stations will be larger, brighter and more spacious, with noticeably larger foot tunnels, better public address systems and modern trains. The lengthy delays suffered by passengers on the older lines as wooden escalators were stripped out and replaced after one of them caught fire with disastrous results at King's Cross station in 1987 taught London Underground a lesson; each JLE station will have lifts and at least three escalators so that there will always be a spare if one is out of service. (A total of 116 new escalators is called for in the designs, compared to the 243 scattered through the rest of the network.) And some of the line's major structures are monumental in scale. North Greenwich station, the key to a hoped-for redevelopment of one of London's most run down and heavily polluted sites, has been designed as a 150 000 ton, 360 metre long 'submarine', almost invisible from the surface but stretching more than half the width of the whole Greenwich peninsula underground.

A project on this huge scale is well beyond the resources of London Underground's normal management structure and once Doherty, with his background of engineering a major phase in the construction of the Hong Kong Underground, had been recruited other specialists quickly joined him. According to the network's managing director, Denis Tunnicliffe, 'Managers of this type are a special breed not retained within our ranks,' and members of the JLE project team were brought in from all over the world. Some had worked with Doherty in Hong Kong, others on the Channel Tunnel. Many of them had experience on the London Ring Main, the gigantic water main, big enough to drive a lorry through, that encircles central London and was the last major tunnelling project completed under the capital. These men were – are – among the élite of the tunnelling world; highly regarded, highly paid, but also highly pressured and expected to complete their work promptly and at the minimum cost.

The twin constraints of time and budget have dictated the engineering of the JLE. According to Doherty, 'You've got to be careful with limits. You can't push them everywhere. And you mustn't push beyond the limits because then you're introducing high risk to a project. The ideal is to generate enough time and flexibility to be able to go to the limit, but we have to deliver this project on time and within budget, so the aim is to balance new ideas with established technology and to go low risk.'

■ **THROUGH THE BOWELS OF THE EARTH** It is technical challenges that most exercise engineers such as Doherty – and the route chosen for the Jubilee Line Extension is full of them. To the north of the Thames, the JLE's tunnels have to weave their way around or through kilometres of crowded soil. Like any great city, and perhaps more than most, London is riddled with subterranean obstacles both natural and man-made, from cellars and bunkers to rivers, gas and water mains and, of course, the Underground network's existing tunnels. To make matters worse, although many of these hazards are mapped, some (chiefly those built during the last century) are not. Their presence means that Doherty's tunnellers have to work in confined spaces, never entirely certain what obstacle might lie in their path.

'Urban tunnelling means working in an environment that makes you feel as if you're living in a goldfish bowl,' said Doherty ruefully. 'When you're working in places like Westminster, you're in the public eye and you're in the eye of the government. There are 650 MPs watching you, and also a local press that has to fill its papers every day. Every time you sneeze, there's a headline.'

As well as passing close to internationally famous structures such as Big Ben and the Palace of Westminster, the JLE project teams are burrowing within 7 metres of the swimming-pool in the basement of the Royal Automobile Club in Pall Mall and face the challenge of tunnelling under Waterloo Station along the route of an existing viaduct supported by century-old deep brick arches. These highly vulnerable structures could not be allowed to settle or crack. The new tunnel is being dug alongside and then under the Northern Line's northbound and southbound lines, which have to be kept running at all times.

The keys to the successful completion of the work are the guidance systems that keep the tunnels running along their planned paths. These machines plot the position and alignment of each workface and make it possible to dig each tunnel to an accuracy measured in millimetres. At the same time, highly sensitive instruments are used to detect any settlement in the earth and in the buildings above as the tunnellers pass through.

The digging of any tunnel, however deep, leaves evidence of its passage on the surface. As the tunnellers advance, their machines compress the ground ahead of them and force earth away and up from the face causing a phenomenon known as 'heaving'. After they have passed, removing the soil leads to subsidence – potentially a major threat to any structure overhead.

Before the first spadeful of Jubilee Line Extension earth was moved, extensive research was conducted by a team from Cambridge University's centre for tunnel technology to establish just how far the buildings along its route moved of their own accord and predicting the possible effects of the 'wave action' caused by the advance of a tunnel underneath them. Thousands of calculations were made and double-checked before sensors were attached to each structure. Each sensor is programmed to trigger should the movement exceed previously determined limits, and each of the groups awarded a JLE contract is obliged to undertake preparatory work to prevent subsidence and keep settlement within strictly defined limits. As a result, Doherty hopes the properties along the line's route will experience ground movement of no more than one millimetre and building cracks of a maximum of 5 millimetres.

Control of subsidence has been made possible by a new technology known as compensation grouting, developed by the Cambridge team and used extensively during the construction of the JLE. The technique involves drilling long, narrow tubes into London Clay above the new Jubilee Line tunnel but below the foundations of buildings along the route so that a fan of tiny shafts up to 50 metres long surrounds any area where subsidence is anticipated. If the team's sensors indicate that ground movement is in fact occurring, concrete is pumped into the tubes to compensate for ground loss and stress release. This stabilizes the ground and limits further movement. A similar technique, 'permeation grouting', protects buildings built on gravels rather than London Clay.

These techniques give Doherty's tunnellers undreamed of control over a hitherto accepted side-effect of their work. The construction of earlier underground lines resulted in the development of cracks up to 180 millimetres wide in some buildings.

'We are at the limit in terms of settlement control,' a satisfied Doherty said, 'and no one has ever done this on this scale before.'

■ **'IT'S NOT NEW AND IT'S NOT AUSTRIAN...'** Tunnelling is not an exact science. All the forward planning, all the millions of pounds spent on research and all the grouting tubes in London could never guarantee against the unexpected – and early one morning in October 1994 the unexpected burst in on the Jubilee Line project team with a vengeance.

Three tunnels under construction for a separate British Airports Authority project on the outskirts of London near Heathrow airport collapsed simultaneously. Although no one was hurt, the scale of the disaster was unprecedented in recent British tunnelling history and the catastrophe caused weeks of delays and frustration for airline passengers. Road links and Underground services faced disruption as large areas were cordoned off at the surface to protect against the dangers of further subsidence while the contractors laboured underground to find the reasons for the collapse.

The Heathrow disaster had serious implications for Doherty and his team, who were tunnelling several kilometres to the east on the early stages of the JLE. Not only was Balfour Beatty, the company that had built the collapsed tunnels, one of the biggest contractors working on the Jubilee Line; the controversial tunnelling method used at the airport had just been introduced on the JLE.

The Heathrow tunnels were being dug using a technique known in engineering circles as NATM – the New Austrian Tunnelling Method. Though neither particularly new (it has been in use now for almost thirty years) nor actually Austrian, NATM (pronounced 'Nattum') had become increasingly popular in Europe because it allows engineers to tunnel rapidly through hard soil and rock without compromising safety while minimizing the dangers of subsidence.

Where traditional shafts were painstakingly and expensively shored with wood, brick or iron bands, tunnels dug using the Austrian Method are supported by quick-drying shotcrete – a mix containing sand, cement and gravel that is sprayed on to the freshly exposed walls to lend them initial support. A separate pressure hose adds an accelerator to the aggregate – just as one might mix an impact adhesive and its hardener – and the quick-setting concrete that is produced lends very early support to a newly tunnelled wall. As the tunnel progresses, the first shotcrete coat is reinforced with secondary coats, wire mesh and lattice girders until the lining is about 150 millimetres thick, and strong enough to allow the work of finishing the tunnel to continue in safety. A completed shotcrete coat is waterproof and includes a thin PVC membrane which isolates stresses between the primary support layer and the curing concrete.

Because shotcrete offers such early support, tunnels dug using NATM can take on a much wider variety of shapes than is normally possible. The system is thus ideal for big jobs such as the excavation of underground stations, which had previously had to be expensively and time-consumingly propped, and for short-distance tunnelling through congested ground where frequent changes of direction are necessary – exactly the conditions that Doherty's team face in London's West End. Most significantly, on a project where schedule and budget are vital, NATM is both cheaper (thanks to the saving in materials) and quicker than the established London Underground method of manufacturing and fitting segmented cast-iron linings to tunnel walls.

Nevertheless, the method was new to the Underground and, although it had been well-tested on the European continent, it had never been used in soft ground in the United Kingdom. For this reason the engineering groups pitching for contracts on the JLE had been obliged to base their proposals for building the tunnels on more conventional methods, although they were allowed to append separate plans for completing part of the work using NATM.

Even at this early stage, however, calculations suggested that switching to the New Austrian Tunnelling Method in tunnels to be built in the centre of London would mean considerable savings in time and money. The JLE team decided to experiment and short sections of tunnel between Westminster and Waterloo were successfully completed using NATM. Surveys showed that the shotcrete support was adequate and that surface settlement remained within the specified limits, and so permission was given to dig larger tunnels using the new method.

Nevertheless, the system remained controversial. Some critics argued that it was not suitable for conditions in London, where solid clay can be interspersed with far more treacherous layers of gravel and quicksand that cannot be penetrated without the help of tunnelling shields; others pointed out that even hiring specialist consultants could not entirely make up for British tunnellers' lack of experience of the method. Doherty therefore had to make a quick decision when he discovered that the NATM tunnels at Heathrow had caved in.

Two tunnels being dug at Heathrow using the New Austrian Tunnelling Method collapsed in October 1994, partly demolishing an office building at the surface. Work on parts of the Jubilee Line Extension was suspended.

'The first time I heard there was a problem was on the radio in my car,' he recalled. 'There were indications of traffic difficulties but there was no indication of what was causing the problem. When I got into my office just before eight o'clock there were rumours that there had been a major problem on the Heathrow tunnel and I made contact with the managing director of the contractor involved to find out what had gone on. He confirmed that the Heathrow tunnels had collapsed but didn't know the reason, so we jointly agreed that we should halt work on the Jubilee Line that day until we knew more about the problems.'

That one day delay stretched into weeks and then into months as the government's Health and Safety Executive launched a detailed investigation into the Heathrow collapse, ignoring the JLE team's protestations that their own NATM work was safe and causing apparently interminable delays in the Westminster area, one of the most significant stretches of the extension – as well as immense and continuing frustration for the tunnelling team. 'There was annoyance that something out of the blue from another contract should actually affect the work that we were doing,' Doherty said. 'The stoppage had a serious impact on morale because of the uncertainty. On a project like this people don't mind problems – they're facing them constantly. It was not knowing when things would be resolved so the men could get back to work that was the major problem.'

Not only morale was threatened by the lengthy stoppage. Although members of the NATM tunnelling team were redeployed to work on other areas of the project, the schedule at its core was threatened. It was the spring of 1995 before permission was given for limited work to recommence on the affected tunnels, and by then Doherty had been forced to consider using other, older methods.

■ **A WORLD OF TUNNELLING TECHNIQUES** As its name implies, the 'new' Austrian tunnelling method succeeded an older way of driving through soft ground which was perfected before steel and machinery changed tunnelling for ever. The old Austrian system was developed to cope with damp and difficult ground and called for the bottom half of a tunnel to be excavated first and heavily propped. The earth to its top and sides would drain into it, making it easier to drive a second tunnel above it, using the roof of the first one to support the props of the second. From there the tunnel was broken out to its full width, starting from the top, and each new section was similarly heavily propped. Because no large spaces were ever left unsupported, the system was strong enough to be used in almost any soil, although tunnels excavated in this way were expensive, thanks to timber costs, and very time-consuming to dig.

During the nineteenth century the Austrian method was widely regarded as the best and safest way of driving through potentially dangerous ground, but similar systems, each suited to a different set of circumstances, were named after the countries in which they were developed. The English system was the most common; it involved driving a horizontal tunnel at roof level and supporting it with heavy crown bars. The tunnel was then widened before being excavated to its full depth. This and the similar Belgian system were complemented by the German method, which reversed the idea and involved building a succession of arches up from floor level, gradually expanding the tunnel to its full height and leaving a central core of earth to be excavated after the shaft had been propped; the American, or block, system of timbering required the construction of timber-lined arches but permitted full-face excavation.

The most expensive and time-consuming system, the Italian, was developed during the driving of the Cristina railway tunnel through the Apennines in 1870 – a project bedevilled by ground as dangerous as any that Doherty has had to contend with. Miners and engineers dug through semi-liquid masses of clay that lacked all cohesion and that slipped over and around each other to exert unbearable pressure on the masonry arches lining the tunnel. When brickwork up to 2 metres thick repeatedly cracked and broke under the strain, the Italians resorted to excavating the lower section of the face and immediately packing it with stonework to create a solid base on which heavy timbers could be erected to support the upper half of the working. The terrible weight of clay forced a gradual reduction in the size of the area that could be worked from 2 metres square to just a metre square, at which point the miners were crouched in a tiny shaft, surrounded on all sides by massive thicknesses of timber.

It took them a year to drive little more than 40 metres in these conditions, and when they had finished the last stretch of the tunnel was only a few millimetres wider than the trains that had to pass through it and was lined by a solid mass of masonry at least 160 centimetres thick on the top, bottom and both sides.

Unhappily for the Jubilee Line tunnelling team, the ground in the East End of London is just as challenging as that encountered in the Cristina tunnel. Here the treacherous Thanet Sands rise close to the surface. Whole machines can be sucked in by quicksand like this, and even if all goes well such dangerous ground slows the rate of progress. North of the river, Doherty's schedule calls for his tunnellers to burrow through up to 170 metres of soil a week, working twenty-four hours a day and five days a week. To the east, the best rate is 75 metres a week, less than half that possible elsewhere.

Even this is impressive, however, given the history of tunnelling in this part of London. The first tunnel under the Thames took sixteen years to complete and cost many men their lives, even though it was dug by a genius.

■ **THE SHIPWORM TUNNEL** At the beginning of the nineteenth century, the port of London was the busiest in the world. Goods that had travelled thousands of miles piled up on the wharves of Limehouse and Rotherhithe before being loaded on to ox carts and heaved creaking through the narrow streets of the docklands towards London Bridge – and the world's biggest traffic jam.

It was not unusual for merchandise from the docks to sit immobile for more than half a day while their drivers waited their turn to pay the toll and cross to the other bank.

The situation was intolerable to a city with London's pride, and it became clear that if private enterprise could succeed in building another crossing closer to the docks there would be a tidy profit to be made in tolls. A bridge was out of the question – nothing could be allowed to deny the tall ships access to the Pool of London – and the thoughts of ambitious men turned to driving a tunnel under the Thames.

The first to attempt to do this were gangs of Cornish miners. They were brought to London by a group of businessmen banded together as the Thames Archway Company who planned a barrel-vaulted passageway from Limehouse to Rotherhithe in London's East End, broad enough to accommodate two lanes of horse-drawn carriages. Work began in the summer of 1807 and the company's men began to drive a pilot tunnel, or driftway, north-westward across the river. The project's chief engineer was a Cornishman, a muscular giant named Richard Trevithick. An able, self-educated man, he had progressed from youthful fame as a wrestler to displaying a dazzling talent for invention. He had harnessed steam power to drive the first self-propelled engine to run on rails, and was convinced that a tunnel could be hacked out under the Thames.

It did not take long for Trevithick to realize he was wrong. His men made fine progress while digging through the London Clay, but once they were under the Thames the ground began to cause them constant anxiety. The tunnel was a cramped 5 feet high by 3 feet wide and water seeped in from the river, 30 feet above their heads, at the rate of 20 gallons a minute. Within this narrow space three miners worked quite literally on their knees. One hewed at the face with his pick, another cleared away the sodden earth and the third shored up the drift with timbers. Working conditions during the six-hour shifts were appalling. The men's bodies were soaked with sweat and river water, no one could stand or stretch and the tunnel was so poorly ventilated that the fetid air sometimes extinguished the candles. Nevertheless, they continued to make progress and by January 1808 Trevithick was able to report that the drift was within 140 feet of the north bank of the Thames and that the tunnel could be completed in a fortnight.

Almost immediately, things began to go badly wrong. The miners hit quicksand, and then water in such quantity that nothing could stop the waterlogged soil from gushing into the driftway and filling it so quickly that the men at the face fled the shaft only just ahead of the flood. Correctly guessing that his tunnel had come too close to an unexpected depression in the bed of the Thames, Trevithick arranged for the hole to be plugged with large bags of clay dumped into the river. To the astonishment of his detractors, this seemingly desperate measure proved successful and the tunnel was pumped dry.

Within days, however, a second flood had occurred and this time the Thames Archway Company had had enough. Its funds were exhausted, its chief engineer was dangerously sick from his exposure to the river water, and its efforts had done nothing but prove that a passage under the river at Rotherhithe exceeded the limits of Regency mining technology.

It took a man of genius to recognize that the picks and shovels and steam pump used by Trevithick were not enough and that a new kind of machine was needed to tunnel beneath London's treacherous river – one that was capable both of preventing the roof and walls from collapsing inward and of holding back the flow of any quicksand or water that might be encountered at the face. This man was Marc Brunel, an *émigré* who had fled his native France during the Revolution and made a name for himself as a prominent engineer. He was a tiny, eccentric man, utterly impractical but an intensely able innovator.

Not long after the failure of the Thames Archway Company he happened to be wandering through the Royal Dockyard at Chatham when his attention was drawn to a rotten piece of ship's timbers discarded on the quay. Idly examining the wood through a magnifying glass, he observed that the plank had been infested with the dreaded *Teredo*, or shipworm, a creature equipped with rasping jaws of

Sailors who had confronted shot and shell feared the dreaded *Teredo*, or shipworm, a mollusc capable of riddling the stoutest warship so full of holes that it became useless for further service. But this most efficient of nature's burrowers provided Marc Brunel with the inspiration for the world's first soft-ground tunnelling machine.

such strength that it is capable of riddling a wooden ship with holes and leaving its timbers so weakened that it is useless for further service. As it burrows, the 'worm' – it is actually a mollusc – shoves pulped wood into its mouth and digests it, excreting a hard, brittle residue which lines the tunnel it has excavated and renders it proof against predators.

Brunel had a fertile mind. Although he had no prior knowledge of, or interest in, tunnelling he realized that the shipworm's devastatingly effective burrowing technique could be adapted to produce an entirely new and far safer way of driving through the ground. His invention, which has been used in one form or another in

Above: Marc Brunel's shield kept miners safe while they tunnelled beneath the Thames.

Right: The chief principles of Brunel's shield were a sturdy iron roof and dozens of wooden poling-boards, held firmly in position by jacks, which were removed one at a time to allow the miners to excavate a letter-box shaped hole a few inches deep in the face. The board was screwed back into position and the next one loosened so the process could be repeated.

almost every major tunnel built during the last 150 years, was the tunnelling shield. It was built from iron frames, which formed a grid that could be pressed against the face of the working and supported a set of horizontal wooden planks, called poling boards, that would hold up the face and prevent it from collapsing into the working. The frames were divided into thirty-six cells, each 3 feet wide and almost 7 feet tall, arranged one on top of another on three levels. The whole machine was 21 feet tall, and could accommodate 120 men. The workface was 850 square feet in size, or sixty-eight times the size of Trevithick's working.

The shield was topped by sturdy iron plates that formed a temporary roof for

the tunnel and protected miners as they worked beneath it. Instead of hewing away at a large and exposed workface, and risking the sort of disaster that had so nearly overtaken Trevithick, the workmen would remove one poling board at a time and hack out a letter-box-shaped hole to a predetermined depth – say 9 inches. Then the plank would be pushed into the hole and screwed back into place before the next timber was removed and the whole process begun again. When the miners in a cell had excavated the earth behind all the boards, the frames were laboriously jacked forward those 9 inches. The 90 ton tunnelling machine could thus move inexorably and safely on while, behind the miners, masons worked rapidly to shore up the newly exposed working by facing the tunnel's circumference with bricks.

Trevithick's driftway was a recent memory at the time Brunel conceived his shield and a tunnel beneath the Thames promised to be a lucrative test of the new invention. Funds for the project were raised through a public subscription and samples taken of the soil beneath the river bed. Brunel was advised to tunnel close to the muddy river bottom, where he could expect to burrow through London Clay, rather than go deeper and risk striking quicksand. When work on the tunnel began in 1825, therefore, the shaft that was sunk in dingy Rotherhithe was only 42 feet deep and the working was planned to pass within 7 feet of the river bed in places.

The hazards of the operation soon became apparent. The shield worked well and the miners at first dug through the predicted clay, but water began to drip into the tunnel before the shaft had even begun to pass under the Thames. Although the influx was filthily polluted – the river was little more than an open sewer for most of London – it was more of a nuisance than a real danger until the summer of 1826, when a fault closed down Brunel's pump and the working was flooded to a depth of 12 feet.

From then on the tunnel proved ever more difficult to dig. Though Brunel's marvellous machine proved able to cope with the sodden mud and dry gravel that his miners encountered as well as with clay, the economies forced on him by shortage of money meant the shaft was poorly drained and ventilated

Marc Brunel revolutionized industry with machines that permitted the introduction of the techniques of mass production and dabbled in bridge-design, naval architecture and tunnelling.

and working conditions within the shield were appalling. The men were poisoned by the river water (one died and many were afflicted by mysterious illnesses from diarrhoea and constant headaches to temporary blindness), half suffocated by exertion and the stagnant air, and tormented by temperatures that could plunge or rise by as much as 30°F within an hour. Finally, in May 1827, when the tunnel was well out under the river, the ground behind the poling boards became so liquid that it forced its way through the gaps between them and gushed into one of the cells with such force that the miner working in it was bowled head over heels and the rest of the men working in the shield could not force their way into his frame in time to staunch the flow. Bitter-tasting, gurgling water rose rapidly and flooded the tunnel as the miners scurried for their ladders and the surface.

Brunel recognized that, like Trevithick's tunnel, his working had passed beneath a cavity in the bed of the Thames, and his solution to the problem was identical: bags of clay. Thousands, containing a total of 20 000 cubic feet of earth, were dumped into the river over the position of the shield, and two weeks after the flood his men began to pump the tunnel dry. The process of draining and cleaning it took four months, and when work started again in November the occasion was marked by a banquet in the tunnel for fifty guests which attracted considerable public comment. Indeed, unremarkable as Brunel's achievements may seem to us, the Thames Tunnel was the principal engineering marvel of its day. Thousands of visitors were permitted to enter the shaft and gaze at the wonderful tunnelling machine on payment of a penny a head. Edward Lear, travelling through the mountains of Calabria, put up one night at a secluded monastery whose unworldly abbot informed his monks: 'England is a very small place, altogether about a third the size of the city of Rome . . . The whole place is divided into two equal parts by an arm of the sea, under which is a great tunnel so that it is all like one piece of dry land.'

Within months of work recommencing the shield was advancing through treacherous ground once more. Early in the morning of 12 January 1828 the miners in one of the top cells were hacking at the face when the earth ahead of them suddenly bulged alarmingly and an unstoppable torrent of water flooded into the tunnel. Once again, the men in the shield had to run for safety, but this time they had left it too late and there were casualties: six miners were drowned. Just as seriously for Brunel, the cost of tipping a further 4500 bags of clay into the Thames to plug this latest hole exhausted his company's inadequate funds. Enough capital was left to pump the tunnel dry and brick up the shield, but attempts to raise new finance failed and tunnelling had to be abandoned.

It took Brunel and his supporters seven years to cajole the government into advancing a loan of £246 000 to allow work on this 'project of national importance' to be completed; and, although the old tunnelling shield was replaced with a new, heavier model that weighed 140 tons and was better able to resist the pressure of the Thames as it swelled with each high tide, six more years of work were required before the tunnel emerged at Wapping on 12 August 1841. During this time work at the face continued around the clock, despite increasingly inadequate ventilation and the dangerous presence of firedamp, which occasionally ignited and enveloped the shield in ghostly flame. Work on the 600 foot tunnel had taken sixteen years and two months, an average rate of progress (allowing for the seven-year lay-off) of only $4\frac{1}{2}$ inches a day – a true measure of the near impossibility of working at, and often beyond, the limits of technology.

Brunel's triumph was only partial. Once again his company's funds were at a low ebb, and though tens of thousands of visitors paid their penny entry fee to walk through what was for many years London's biggest tourist attraction, the money this raised was hardly sufficient to pay interest on the government's loan. There was never enough to complete the approaches to the tunnel and make it possible for horse-drawn vehicles to use it. Instead, the passageways were filled with souvenir-sellers by day and by the city's homeless each night. For the penny toll, vagrants could bed down under Brunel's arches in what became known as the 'Hades Hotel'.

The Thames Tunnel achieved a measure of real usefulness only when the underground railway came to London in the 1860s. It was bought by the East London Railway in 1869 and, on inspection, was found to be in such excellent condition that it was immediately pressed into service carrying steam-driven trains at first along the Brighton line to the coast and later from Wapping to New Cross in south London. The

The man who took the tunnelling shield and turned it into a machine still recognizable today was James Greathead, a South African who deserves to rank with Brunel as one of the founding fathers of modern soft-ground tunnelling.

tunnel became and remains part of the London Underground network – the only line so far to the east until the advent of the Jubilee Line Extension.

■ **SHIELDS AGAINST DISASTER** The rectangular tunnelling shield was only the first step in the development of the sort of shield technology used on the Jubilee Line Extension, and the concept was significantly developed when the successor to Brunel's tunnel was driven under the Thames twenty-five years later. Although the enthusiasm of potential contractors was dented by memories of the hideous problems faced by Brunel's miners – and the singular lack of commercial success enjoyed by the Thames Tunnel – the London firm of P.W. Barlow eventually agreed to undertake the work in 1865 using a new shield that had been patented by Peter Barlow himself.

The principal difference between Barlow's machine and Brunel's was that the new shield was circular in profile and – like every significant successor – it did not depend on teams of masons to line the tunnel with bricks. Instead, miners working behind it fitted pre-fabricated iron rings, each about 18 inches wide and forged in three sections, to the freshly dug walls. As well as providing superior protection to the tunnel, they were easier and quicker to fit than masonry. Similar sections are still fitted to many shafts dug today.

The new Thames tunnel, which ran between Tower Hill and Tooley Street, was a pedestrian footway and Barlow's shield was far smaller than the one invented by Brunel – a mere 8 feet in diameter. One miner would step into it through a small hexagonal opening in its centre and hack at the soil until there was room enough for a second man, and then a third, to join him. Barlow employed proportionately fewer men than Brunel, and because he and his principal engineer, a young Cape Colony man named James Greathead, had the good fortune to be driving through London Clay, work on the tunnel was completed in only nine months – their shield clawed through about 50 inches of earth each day, a dozen times faster than Brunel's machine – and at a cost of only £20 000. Like Brunel's shaft, the Tower Hill tunnel is still in use, though it now conveys water pipes and cables, rather than people, under the Thames.

His experience of subaqueous tunnelling fired Greathead to further innovation, and in the last quarter of the nineteenth century he developed a system of

The Greathead tunnelling shield was a substantial improvement on Brunel's design. It was circular rather than rectangular in shape and required far fewer miners. Perhaps the most significant advance, however, was the introduction of pre-fabricated iron rings for lining the freshly excavated tunnel. These plates are often used in new London Underground tunnels.

tunnelling that is still used today. The South African introduced a number of key improvements that made future machines far safer than those used by Brunel. If a shield hit water or quicksand it was possible to close a watertight bulkhead at the rear to prevent the tunnel flooding and the consequent necessity of laboriously re-sealing it and pumping it clear. Sealing and supporting the freshly dug tunnel was speeded by the invention of the grout pan, which used compressed air to force grout into the lining. In addition, hydraulic rams were used to move the machines forward, making progress smoother and faster.

Further innovations followed as the London Underground network grew. In 1897 an engineer named John Price, working on the construction of the Central Line, devised one of the first practicable powered tunnelling machines, the precursor of many of the monsters used on the JLE. Like the Brunel and Greathead shields, his device filled the whole cross-section of the tunnel. It was electrically powered and built around a rotating cutting-head which tore away at the soil at the face. Four rotating arms which extended from the head to the edge of the bore swept muck into a chute and funnelled it backwards. The machine was a success, and Price was able to correct its principal faults – it could not turn corners, and tended to swing in the direction in which its raking arms rotated. An improved model was soon boring up to 180 feet of tunnel a week on the new Northern Line.

But tunnelling successfully through stable clay on land was one thing; boring under water remained quite another. In soil beneath rivers and seas there was always the danger of hitting 'running ground' (sand) or, worse, 'flowing ground' (water and water-bearing muck). For many years the only practicable solution was itself potentially as deadly as quicksand: compressed air.

■ **BONE ROT AND BLOW HOLES** Compressed air offers miners two great advantages: it drives water back from the face in flowing ground, so that the men can excavate dry sand and gravel rather than a semi-liquid mass; and it supports the face, preventing it from crumbling in on the workmen. It had first been used in tunnels by Greathead, but similar technology was still in use when the Clyde tunnel – the project on which Hugh Doherty first fell in love with tunnelling – was built under Glasgow in the 1960s.

'It was my first tunnelling job,' Doherty recalled. 'I was eighteen at the time, studying civil engineering at Strathclyde. A colleague of mine had been offered a job in the tunnel, but he had a lot of difficulty with his sinuses, and he struggled in the compressed air. I thought I'd give it a go, I passed the medical, and I was able to start work.

'To work in compressed air you had to go into a pressurized chamber. You walk through a very small door into a small chamber and it's very claustrophobic, sweaty, cramped and muddy. You feel a pressure building up on your ears. You've got to be careful you don't have a cold, because if you do you can burst your eardrums – and you can't whistle, that's one of the things that you find. The first thing you notice when you get into the air chamber at the face is that it's very hot and the miners are all stripped off and sweating. The pressure was of the order of one and a half atmospheres – that's 30-plus pounds per square inch. Of course when you come out you have to be decompressed for a long time, too, which reduces productivity. It's very sticky – not everyone enjoys it.'

Seven hundred and forty men worked on the Clyde project, burrowing only 4 metres below the bed of Scotland's great river, and three of them died: tunnelling conditions, even in the 1960s, were primitive by the most modern standards. There was little in the way of personal protective gear; miners still wore cloth caps rather than hard hats, and few of them had any real conception of what compressed air could do. There were cases of the bends, an agony usually suffered only by divers who have surfaced so quickly that nitrogen remains trapped in their joints, causing them to expand painfully. But the true cost of building the tunnel is still being counted, for recent studies have shown that as many as 125 of the tunnellers now suffer from necrosis, or rotting of the bones – a refinement that occurs when air pressure affects the blood supply to the joints. It is a stealthy disease whose presence is not immediately felt. Indeed claims for compensation from the miners affected are still being lodged today.

Bone rot was not the only danger that confronted tunnellers using compressed air. The pressure exerted on the tunnel walls was such that the roof could blow out in weak ground, as happened during the driving of a New York Metro rapid transit tunnel under the East River in 1905. As it came close to the river bed, compressed air blew a hole in its roof and a miner named Richard Creegan, one of the eight 'sandhogs' working in the shield, was sucked upwards into the hole. For a moment he stuck there, with his body in the silt of the river bed and his legs kicking wildly in the tunnel; then, as his colleagues rushed to haul him back down, the pressure built to the point where he was shot upwards through $4\frac{1}{2}$ metres of water to the surface – where he was rescued, unharmed, by a group of astonished boatmen. A similar incident occurred in Glasgow, though on this occasion the miner's mates formed a human chain and managed to drag him back below as the compressed air howled out around them, up into the river. The waters of the Clyde forced their way down into the tunnel and two of the other men working in the chamber drowned.

The lessons learned on the Clyde tunnel were serious ones. Revised guidelines governing the amount of time workmen could spend in the pressure chamber threatened to make subaqueous tunnelling uneconomic; the men of each shift would spend more time decompressing than actually working at the face. A new idea was needed, and it came to British engineer, John Bartlett.

Bartlett's inspiration came from a study of landslides in areas where the soil was made from what is known as Bentonite clay. Investigations had shown that they occurred after heavy rain, when the clay had absorbed so much water that it spontaneously liquefied when subjected to shock. Once a landslide had roared down into the valley below the clay stabilized and reverted to its old solid form.

Bartlett decided to use this unexpected property in a tunnelling machine. He devised a system of pumping high-pressure Bentonite slurry against a workface; the pressure and shock was enough to force water back from a loose and dangerous soil and simultaneously transform the Bentonite itself into a liquid that supported the face. Rotating cutter arms then swept across the now dry soil, which crumbled and could be pumped away together with the liquid mud – which was separated out and recycled. But despite a successful trial conducted in 1972 under New Cross in south London, in ground similar to that encountered by Brunel, local investment dried up and it was left to the Japanese to develop efficient Bentonite machines capable of boring the eastern portion of the Jubilee Line Extension.

Modern Japanese tunnel technology is one of the most positive legacies of the Second World War. The country's ruined cities were rebuilt from the underground up, giving local tunnellers extensive experience in all types of ground. Today Japan is home to the world's longest tunnel, the 30 kilometre long Seikan between the

Modern tunnel-boring machines such as this example built by Kawasaki use rotating arms fitted with dozens of individual picks to claw their way through the soil. Their operators are protected by airlocks and other safety systems.

islands of Honshu and Hokkaido. It took twenty years to complete and was bored through a wide variety of rock, including soft, sandy mudstone at its centre. Here, one 500 metre section took four years to dig. During the 1980s engineers working for Kawasaki succeeded in perfecting mud injection shields suitable for work in south-east London and it is these monsters that have been set to tunnel from Rotherhithe north to the Isle of Dogs, back under the river to Greenwich, and then north again towards Stratford.

The Kawasaki shields work by balancing mud injection and earth extraction to keep the workface under constant pressure. Excess pressure is released through a screw conveyor at the centre, and a number of safety devices are fitted – the machine can even shut off a workface completely, protecting the men in the tunnel behind it, if it hits freak conditions that threaten a disaster. Even so, maintenance remains a dangerous business. If the cutter head breaks down – as it sometimes does – the pressure at the face has to be maintained to prevent a collapse while a tunneller enters through an airlock and labours in the compressed air to repair the head. A lengthy job means time in a decompression chamber for the engineer in question. These earth pressure balance machines, or EPBs, remain at the cutting edge of tunnelling technology.

The schedules constructed by Doherty and his JLE project team managed to engineer a fitting hand over between this new technology and the old. As Sharon and Tracey, Kawasaki's twin EPBs, chewed their way under the Thames heading for Canary Wharf, Brunel's tunnel was being closed for major repairs, 150 years after it had opened. The brick arches that supported it had finally begun to leak, letting the river back into the passageways it had flooded so many decades before. But such was the strength of the Victorian tunnellers' work that Brunel's tunnel has already been reopened. When the Jubilee Line Extension is completed, the two tunnels, one ancient, one modern, will run side by side and will serve the East End of London into the twenty-first century.

CHAPTER THREE

BIG

magine an aircraft bigger than the biggest passenger airliner that has ever flown. An aircraft that could carry twice as many people as a jumbo jet, and still cross the Pacific Ocean in a single hop. A plane with seats along the whole lengths of two decks, not just one, that has been built by brilliant engineers using the most advanced computers and incorporates dozens of technological breakthroughs. Such an aeroplane does not exist – not yet – but within a few years, if all goes well, it will. It is called the Airbus A3XX, and it will be huge, and powerful, and safe. But it is a fair bet that few people will board it without experiencing at least a hint of trepidation.

We are right to be afraid of flying. Not so much because air travel is dangerous – each of us is safer, statistically, on board an aircraft than we are in our own homes – but because a commercial airliner takes us into a world of unbearable extremes. When your aircraft reaches its cruising altitude you will be maybe 8 miles high and sitting in a pressurized fuselage blown up like a balloon to provide you with a co-coon of air; outside, the atmosphere is far too thin to breathe and the temperature is $-50°C$, so cold that without an insulating layer the window would burn your hand if you touched it. True, the aeroplane is the product of decades of trial (and, sometimes, error) and thousands of hours of computer-aided design, drawing-board calculations and structural wind-tunnel testing; but while an architect may routinely build a skyscraper that is ten times stronger than it needs to be, the uncompromising demands of aerodynamics, fuel efficiency and airline profit have combined to ensure that the safety margin on board a passenger aircraft is not 1000 per cent but 50 per cent.

That this small margin is generally sufficient is a tribute to those who have overcome the problems of heavier-than-air flight – problems that frequently had no parallel in the history of engineering. Successful powered flight required not just the invention of powerful lightweight engines and an understanding of the principles of lift and drag, but also a practical knowledge of how to control a craft moving not in two dimensions but in three, and one that was therefore also liable to roll, pitch and yaw.

This knowledge was the key to successful flight. The Wright brothers were not, as is popularly supposed, the first men to fly; that honour probably belongs to a Frenchman named Clement Ader, who catapulted himself skywards in a primitive monoplane as early as 1890 and crashed to earth 50 metres away. The Wrights'

Previous page: The Russian Antonov AN-225 is the biggest aircraft currently flying.

achievement was much more significant: controlled flight. Of all the men reaching for the skies at the turn of the century only Orville and Wilbur – practical men, bicycle mechanics – had devoted endless hours to repetitive experiments with flaps and rudders, and developed their skills by flying manned kites.

The lead that the Wright brothers' skills gave them was so great that they remained the only fliers in the world for several years after their initial triumph. From the moment that others joined them in the air, however, the new science of aeronautics shot forward with astonishing speed. Little more than ten years after the brothers' first short flight aeroplanes were fighting one another over the trenches of Flanders, and within twenty it was possible to board a large passenger plane at Croydon airport and be flown, in some comfort, to Paris.

The first passenger aircraft were in fact built immediately before the outbreak of the First World War and of these perhaps the most remarkable was Le Grand, the brainchild of the Russian-born aeronautical engineer Igor Sikorsky. It was the world's first four-engined plane and also the first to combine an enclosed cockpit with passenger accommodation. Sikorsky – who later took American citizenship and lived long enough and thought deeply enough to become a pioneer of giant helicopters in the 1950s – personally piloted Le Grand on its maiden voyage across Russia in 1913, and within a few months the plane had successfully carried eight passengers on a two hour flight. Their accommodation was more luxurious than even first class passengers can hope to enjoy today: it included the use of a sofa, table, wardrobe and curtains, as well as the first airborne WC, all within a compartment 1.8 metres wide and less than 6 metres long.

Le Grand was a success and was in many ways the model on which all future passenger aircraft were based. In its final form it could fly at up to 90 kilometres per hour (not too fast, even for the day), had a 27 metre wingspan and weighed, fully loaded, 4 tons. Its largest contemporaries spanned little more than 15 metres and weighed only 2 tons. It was a truly limit-busting aircraft. Although its critics argued that it was only its rather poor performance that prevented it

Igor Sikorsky began his career building bi-planes in tsarist Russia and ended it as America's leading designer of helicopters.

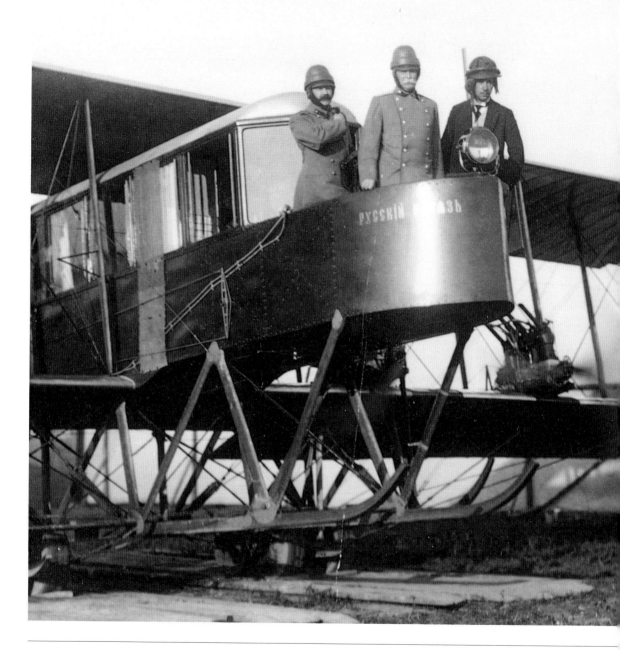

Le Grand was the world's first four-engined plane and the progenitor of all large passenger aircraft. It had a wingspan of 27 metres and flew at a sedate 90 kilometres per hour. Only one version was ever built – and was destroyed on the ground when an engine fell off an aircraft that was flying overhead and plummeted on to it.

from tearing itself to pieces in the air, it was actually destroyed not in a crash but on the ground when an engine from an aircraft flying directly overhead dropped on to it.

Sikorsky followed Le Grand with another aircraft, the Ilya Mourometz. It was successfully converted into a heavy bomber and reconnaissance aircraft during the First World War, and ever since then passenger aircraft have provided the templates for military planes, and wartime bombers have become civil aircraft when peace breaks out. Indeed, a jumbo jet and a B–52 bomber have far more in common than the B–52 has with a sleek jet fighter, since each is designed to carry the largest possible weight great distances, rather than for speed and manoeuvrability. So it was that, after 1945, the American Dakota military transport became the beloved DC–3, which remains in service with a number of South American airlines today. More recently Boeing 707s, designed as passenger aircraft, have been converted into airborne command centres and 747s are used to ferry space shuttles to their launch pads. The biggest aircraft currently flying, the Russian Antonov AN–225 six-engined jet transport, has a wingspan of 88 metres, an 80 metre fuselage and cargo capacity of up to 250 tons. A military plane, it might have made a formidable passenger aircraft were it not for the fact that, perversely, civil aircraft have to be far tougher, more robust and reliable than their air force counterparts. A military transport will spend only a tiny fraction of its time airborne, and its pilots will never have to worry about the comfort of passengers and only rarely about the logistical problems of disembarking and then loading as quickly as possible. An airliner, on the other hand, must be refuelled, reprovisioned and back in the air within minutes of landing if it is to pay its way. It must fly for months between major overhauls, and its maintenance costs must be minimal.

Above all, it must be designed and built with the needs of its customers, the airlines, firmly in mind.

■ **JUMBO JETS** The Bristol Brabazon was Britain's attempt to turn a big bomber project into a civil airliner. It started life in 1941 to meet a government requirement for a plane capable of hauling $4\frac{1}{2}$ tons of bombs almost 6500 kilometres, far enough to strike deep into the heart of Europe. A year later, however, it was decided to start planning for a post-war world. A committee chaired by Lord Brabazon was set up to investigate the probable requirements for civil aircraft, and someone pointed out that a converted Bristol bomber would make an impressive transatlantic passenger plane, capable of flying non-stop to New York.

By 1946, design work on the planned airliner was almost complete. As built, it was the biggest aircraft ever made in Britain – an all-metal monoplane with eight engines, which were fitted in pairs and supplied with contra-rotating propellers and an enormous – 70 metre – wingspan. BOAC, one of the forerunners of present-day British Airways, laid down specifications for 100 seats and a large pressurized cabin. However, the cabin was so much bigger than anything produced in Britain up to then that it was never completed and the plane took to the skies unpressurized. Building this remarkable aircraft became something of a national passion, but it took the Bristol Aeroplane Company a long time – ten years – to progress from conception to a production model. The prototype flew, to great excitement, in 1949, but for all its technical accomplishments the aircraft was a commercial failure. Gradually it became clear that Britain had built a plane without a customer, one that had taken so long to design and test that it had been overtaken by the arrival of new American-built jetliners. Even BOAC preferred to buy its aircraft elsewhere.

The Brabazon taught the British aircraft industry a tough lesson: that there is no point in building a new plane unless you are certain it is what your customers want and that you can sell it. It was a lesson that was learned on the other side of the Atlantic, where the Boeing corporation of Seattle was also switching from building heavy bombers to commercial planes. The company had gained its experience building air force monsters such as the B–29 Superfortress and the post-war B–47 – the plane which introduced the swept wing that turned out to be the key to high-speed jet flight. Eventually, though, it came to dominate large passenger aircraft construction, thanks partly to the close links that developed between its president, Bill Allen, and Juan Trippe, the dictatorial boss of Pan American Airways. Allen built Boeing's increasingly successful 'seven' series aircraft – the 707, the 727 and the 737 – and Trippe bought them. Rivals' fear of mighty Pan-Am meant that Boeing was able to sell the same planes to other airlines.

Even so, by the mid-1960s Trippe was beginning to think in terms of much bigger aircraft. With passenger volumes predicted to grow by 200 per cent over the next fifteen years he was sure he could fill them, and during a fishing holiday in Alaska he and his old friend Allen talked themselves into building a new Boeing:

the 747. They had no idea what it would look like, but were determined that it would have at least 400 seats, double the capacity of the old 707. When Allen's engineers told him it could not be done, he told them to do it anyway.

His decision traumatized the company for years. There were endless engineering problems to solve: how many engines would the big plane need, where should they be placed, and should the passengers (or freight, for the 747 was intended to have a cargo variant) be accommodated on one deck or two? Slowly the answers emerged. The 747 was given an extra-wide 6 metre (20 foot) fuselage,

Adapted from a wartime bomber design, the Bristol Brabazon was meant to be Britain's answer to the American domination of the post-war air-lanes. An engineering triumph in its own right, it was outclassed by the new jet airliners.

broad enough to sit ten economy class passengers in a single row; it received four big Pratt & Whitney engines, slung under wings that had a span of 60 metres (200 feet). And it flew.

Development of the 747 cost Boeing more than a billion dollars and dug the company so far into a financial pit that it came close to collapse. But when the 747 started to sell, it sold well – it broke even in 1978 when 400 had been ordered – and kept on selling, year after year, until this engineering marvel became by far the biggest profit-maker Boeing had ever known. It helped to drive Douglas, the Seattle company's most feared competitor, into the second division of civil aircraft manufacturers and by the late 1970s Boeing was probably the only company left in the first division.

However, by concentrating on the 747 and on transoceanic routes, Boeing left itself vulnerable to an attack from behind. It had happened to the company once before when Douglas, rather than its Seattle rival, had spotted a demand for small passenger jets to shuttle between cities within the United States and developed the DC–9 to exploit it. In the 1970s it happened again. This time the challenge came from Europe, where an improbable coalition of manufacturers from France, Germany, Britain and Spain – including British Aerospace – banded together to form a consortium called Airbus Industrie with headquarters in Toulouse. It designed a medium range plane, the A300, to compete with Boeing's proposed 777, and in the time it took the Americans to decide on a design and get its new aircraft into production, Airbus sold almost 400 of its new aeroplanes. Over the last two decades, the European consortium has become as feared a competitor to the American company as Douglas had been, ranking a comfortable second to Boeing in size. But it still has nothing to rival the jumbo jet, which has earned its makers profits that can be measured in hundreds of millions of dollars.

For Airbus and its competitors, the whole history of passenger aviation has been driven by three factors: further, faster, bigger. In the 1920s and 1930s the principal problem was how to increase the range of aircraft, particularly in the United States where air travel was challenging the supremacy of the train; by the end of this period, transatlantic passenger flights were possible. In the 1940s and 1950s jet engines emerged to revolutionize the speed with which it was possible to move from A to B; the 1960s and 1970s saw the introduction of large, wide-bodied airliners such as the 747 series and also of Concorde, the world's first supersonic passenger plane. By the end of the 1980s, however, important limits had been reached. Now that it will soon be possible – just – to fly from Britain to Australia in a single hop, there is little point in building planes with a greater range. And environmental concerns have made it impossible to operate supersonic aircraft over land, leaving Concorde the transatlantic and transpacific routes but barring it and any successors from the potentially lucrative Europe-to-Asia and intra-Asian routes. Meanwhile, air traffic is expected to grow by 5 per cent a year, every year, for the foreseeable future. Airports will not grow so fast, and the number of landing slots available will remain limited.

Airbus is convinced that its best option is to make its products bigger, both to cope with the steadily rising demand for seats and to offer airlines the lowest possible cost-per-passenger and so the ability to compete in an increasingly price sensitive and cut-throat market.

■ **THE AIRBUS ROUTE** None of Boeing's rivals has yet competed successfully against the 747. The plane that nearly bankrupted the Seattle giant is now indisputably its greatest product, too expensive for any one company to mimic. Perhaps only a consortium – and one enjoying some government-backed loans, to boot – could hope to beat the jumbo jet. Even Airbus Industrie hesitated before taking up the challenge. It was 1987, and the company had launched a range of five models, from the little A320 up to the four-engined A340, before Airbus began to think seriously about the requirements its customers would have in the twenty-first century and recognized with increasing certainty that its next plane should be a giant.

It decided that if the new Airbus Industrie aircraft – code-named A3XX – was to be worthwhile it should not be simply a 747 clone or just a little bigger than its rival, but a plane that made the kind of leap into the future that had helped Boeing to success with its jumbo jet. In the cautious world of commercial aviation, new aircraft are reckoned ambitious if they are 5 or 10 per cent more efficient than their predecessors. The A3XX is designed to cut the airlines' key statistic, direct operating costs per passenger, by between 15 and 20 per cent – enough to ensure the continued fall in the cost of air travel in real terms. If Airbus Industrie's projections are correct there could be a market for between 500 and 850 such planes up to the year 2014

which, at around $200 million per plane (slightly more than the cost of a jumbo jet), means total potential revenues of anything up to $170 billion.

Even to a company the size of Airbus Industrie, the $8 billion development cost of the new project will be colossal, and far more than that of any of its previous programmes. Most of the money should come in the form of cash flowing from predicted sales of 150 to 200 of its existing aircraft per year, but some will have to be sought from partners. One possibility is an Asian manufacturer, but another – unlikely as it seems on the face of it – is an alliance with Boeing. This prediction is based on the appreciation that Seattle cannot allow its European rival to get too much of a head start if the new market turns out to be a real one, and that there may not be enough room for two giant planes to compete head to head.

The man in charge of a project that could well mean the difference between life and death for the Airbus Industrie consortium is a genial, gloriously moustachioed Frenchman named Jean-Jacques Huber. An aeronautical engineer who has more than twenty years experience with the company, Huber has worked on all the major families of aircraft Airbus Industrie has produced, but his new job as manager of the A3XX project is without question the most daunting he has ever had – one packed with so many challenges that he estimates the new plane may not actually enter service until 2003, the year he himself is due to retire.

For Huber, A3XX is the project that vindicates his choice of profession. 'I was not so sure until a couple of years ago that becoming an aeronautical engineer was a good decision,' he recalled. 'Of the guys I originally studied with, one is now selling cars, others are in railways, some are working in foreign countries, so there was a lot of choice. But in the last few years we have had the chance to build four different sorts of aircraft. It was a very good time, and now there is the opportunity to be there with a plane for the next generation.'

■ **THE BIGGEST BIRD** The A3XX project is full of fascination for a man like Huber and he admitted that, 'The challenge is a big one. Each new aircraft built has to be more sophisticated and more efficient than the one before – simply because airlines want to carry more passengers at lower cost. But this is an extraordinary project, because with this size of airliner you face limits wherever you turn. It must be able to use all the main airports around the world, it must have a range of at

Top: A simulation of the Airbus A3XX gives some idea of its great size. Although no longer than a Boeing 747, it is far bulkier and will carry passengers along two decks.

Above: The Boeing 747 jumbo jet nearly bankrupted its manufacturer before turning into the most versatile, ubiquitous – and lucrative – civil aircraft of the last quarter-century.

least 14 000 kilometres and, most important of all, it must carry passengers for a considerably lower cost than any plane now flying.'

The management of the project has to be as sophisticated as the engineering, involving as it does co-ordinating work by four very different partners. Industrial considerations mean that Airbus lacks a central production facility: Britain makes the wings of the biggest Airbus planes, the front part of the fuselage comes from France, the rear from Germany, and the tail is shipped in from Spain. Then there are the potential customers, each wanting to be heard, each with its own requirements – some demand maximum range so the plane can hop the Pacific, others suggest greater freight capacity, still others want more comforts for passengers. Airbus Industrie will have to view the aircraft as a whole rather than as a series of problems each awaiting its own solution.

Huber's first step was to commission research. There were a thousand questions to answer. How big must the wing be to support the passenger load? Are existing engines powerful enough to fly the big bird, or will a new generation of power plants be required? Can the tailplane be made small enough to fit into existing hangars? There are no more than two or three years to find the solutions to every problem if the A3XX is to meet Huber's unofficial target of flying for the first time at the Farnborough Air Show in the year 2002.

One of the men he is hoping will help to find these solutions is Dieter Schmitt, for a while Airbus Industrie's head of future technology and now Chief Engineer New Projects. Schmitt is a worried man: 'The technology will be crucial. For example, if we can't improve the efficiency of the wing then the whole plane will not be possible. In nearly every area of design there will need to be quantum leaps; we will have to use new materials and advanced systems. Everything that's important in a small plane will become absolutely vital in one this size.'

Schmitt's problems start with the main body of the A3XX. Every new passenger aircraft is built around a pressurized fuselage, even though the passenger compartment within it may be one of the last things to be designed. Long years of experience have shown that a circular or slightly oval shape is best for resisting air pressure and reducing drag. During preliminary studies for the new plane, the Airbus team looked at adding width by designing a fuselage that would be constructed from the intersection of two circles. However, tests showed it would not have been strong enough for many years of safe operation miles up in the sky and so they adopted an oval design.

Even so, the sheer scale of the new fuselage is remarkable. The first thing a passenger boarding the A3XX will notice is the enormous number of seats. The earliest models to be produced are likely to carry up to 850 people in an all-economy layout or 570 in three classes. This gigantic capacity will be possible because the plane is intended, unlike its predecessors, to be a double-decker. This unusual configuration has been proposed before, in the original designs of the 747 – six seats in a row on the upper deck, and five below – but in the end Boeing chose to give its jumbo jets wide bodies rather than an extra floor, and provided only a small, first class, cabin on the top deck. The A3XX is slightly wider than a 747 and will have up to eight seats in a row in the upper area and ten abreast in the lower one.

Indeed, it is possible that some airlines will order variants with not two but three decks open to passengers. Airbus Industrie's feasibility studies have shown that it would be possible to replace one of the two cargo holds below the main deck with additional facilities without significantly reducing cargo and baggage allowances. The space is most likely to be used to increase passenger comfort by providing additional facilities. Airbus's proposals include a health suite or a cinema, but some airlines have even more ambitious plans. Richard Branson's Virgin Atlantic Airways, which has made its name by concentrating on passenger service, has suggested a children's area or a smoking section completely separate from the non-smoking sections above.

According to Branson, 'In the future you'll have a bar with a hostess serving drinks, lounges, in-flight entertainment systems which give you a choice of fourteen different channels, swipe cards that will let you do your shopping on the same system, television channels beamed into the planes, phones. But I think the thing that most of our passengers would really like, something which we'd be able to offer with big planes, is proper beds. They'll have seats which won't have quite as much space as they currently have, but then they'll be able to come down to a place where they can stretch out completely flat, be given their teddy bear and go to sleep. I think that's the dream for most business travellers.'

So while one team of Airbus engineers ponders the design of the A3XX's exterior, another must devote itself to modelling the interior, balancing increasing demands for passenger comforts such as seat-back video screens and arm-rest telephones against the need to squeeze the maximum possible number of paying customers into the aircraft. Seat width and seat pitch are vital; changing the angle of the seat-backs by as little as a few degrees can mean fitting in two or three extra rows of seats.

Milt Heinemann, for years the Boeing company's leading 'passenger engineer', once persuaded his colleagues to add an extra 6 inches to the length of a fuselage because he had calculated that this small increase would allow him to squeeze in another half-dozen seats.

The potential to pack hundreds of extra passengers into the A3XX creates numerous additional problems. The investment that airlines are required to make in modern aircraft has created enormous pressure to achieve a fast turnaround time. On short-haul routes, luggage must be unloaded and planes serviced, refuelled, resupplied and cleaned in no more than 100 minutes, and that means disembarking passengers as quickly as possible. An A3XX with 850 people on board must take no longer to clear – and safety regulations still insist that it must be possible for every passenger to be evacuated within ninety seconds of a crash landing, through only half of the doors.

'It's clear,' Huber explained, 'that for an aircraft with more or less the same length as a 747 to have 40 per cent more passengers, you have first to offer more doors. With the double-deck configuration we could offer this. We will have nine exits on one side, each wide enough for two people to go through at once so it is possible to evacuate 110 people from each door in ninety seconds. It is part of the challenge because there are very strict regulations on the organization of doors – it's not possible, for example, to have more than 18 metres between two doors, and there must be some equilibrium in the cabin layout as well.'

■ **WINGS AND THINGS** Once the number of passengers to be carried has been decided and the fuselage sketched out, it is possible to build wings capable of lifting them into the sky. Wings are the feature that most passengers wonder at when they board a big aircraft. They tend to look flimsy in comparison with the bulk of the fuselage and in flight they seem to flap and buckle. In fact, they are very carefully shaped pieces of advanced engineering. Every part of their design must be carefully tested in a wind tunnel like the 1000 kilometre per hour facility at Bedford used by British Aerospace, each degree of sweep calculated and every kilogram of surplus weight eliminated. But the most important factor is lift.

Lift is what keeps an aeroplane flying. It is produced when an engine pushes an inclined plane – the wing – through the air. The air flowing over the upper surface goes faster than that underneath and this results in a drop in air pressure on the top of the wing. The consequence keeps the aircraft industry in business: the higher pressure under the wing pushes the aeroplane upwards and skywards.

But when an inclined plane or aerofoil produces lift it also, unavoidably, creates drag – potentially enough to slow an aircraft significantly and make it inefficient and more liable to create noise and pollution. One of the key technologies for ultra-high-capacity aircraft is drag reduction, and Airbus Industrie has been researching what is known as 'laminar flow control'. When a plane is in flight a laminar, or smooth, flow of air around it is needed to minimize drag, but along parts of a plane's surface – like the leading edge of the wing – the flow is normally disturbed or turbulent. Several researchers have been working on ways of extending the area of laminar flow around an aircraft the size of the A3XX. Among them is Professor Ian Poll at Manchester University's department of aeronautics. He has developed a scheme for using lasers to drill literally millions of tiny 'pores', each no more than 50 microns in diameter, into the leading edge of a wing and then sucking the disturbed air through these holes.

The system has functioned perfectly in the laboratory, and if it can be made to work in the air, it could reduce drag by anything up to 35 per cent and the A3XX's fuel burn by perhaps 15 to 20 per cent, increasing the aircraft's range and making it considerably quieter and far more efficient to run.

The merits of the new scheme are still under debate. Critics within the Airbus Industrie consortium fear that small particles of debris or rain could clog the pores and prevent the system working and, at this stage, it is more likely to be used on the tail and engine pods than on the wings, where most drag is generated. Poll, however, is certain that laminar flow control can be perfected with the

Jean-Jacques Huber, the engineer at Airbus Industrie who is responsible for the A3XX super jumbo jet.

help of new laser drilling technology that has only just recently been developed.

'Drag is one of the barrier problems for these large aircraft,' he said. 'The operating costs and pollution characteristics have got to be minimized because this is a twenty-first century aircraft and we have to think ahead. The bigger the aircraft, the bigger the potential for drag improvement, so on an ultra-high-capacity aircraft this kind of technology can have a very big impact.'

The A3XX's wings will be very unusual even if they are not fitted with a laminar flow system. Thanks to the work of British Aerospace, Airbus Industrie's United Kingdom partner, each will be among the most carefully engineered structures ever built. A single pair will have a span of almost 80 metres, 12 metres greater than that of a jumbo jet, and will be far too big to be moved in one piece, even using the gigantic cargo transporters owned by Airbus Industrie. Instead, they will be built and shipped in sections, then slotted together using thick aluminium spars each more than 30 metres long – close to the limit of what the company's raw material manufacturers can supply – and machined to leave a profile that is aerodynamically efficient but which also gives strength and the necessary rigidity. The 20 metre outer section of each wing will be shaped from a huge piece of carbon fibre, the largest yet incorporated into any commercial aircraft, which will add strength while offering a significant saving in weight.

Another fundamental limit confronts aeronautical engineers as they build bigger and bigger aircraft. In the very largest planes – bigger even than the A3XX – the lift pushing the plane up will be squared in proportion to the area of the wings, whereas the aircraft's weight, pushing it down, is cubed, a function of its volume. Doubling the size of a really large aircraft therefore results in an eight-fold increase in its weight, while the lift supplied by its wings experiences only a four-fold increase. The bigger plane's wings will have to be made proportionately larger to provide the necessary lift, and this principle has led to the creation of limit-busting designs that do away with ordinary fuselages altogether – the so-called flying wings.

The first examples, built by the American engineer Jack Northrop, were flown as early as 1928, and his company retained an interest in the idea for the next fifty years. Northrop's calculations showed that by eliminating an aircraft's fuselage and tail – the parts that create an important part of its drag – a flying wing could fly as much as 40 per cent further than a conventional plane, and almost 20 per cent

Jack Northrop's **XB55** flying wing took to the air in 1946 and was a radical departure from conventional aircraft design.

Although it was an engineering success, the concept still has to gain acceptance from airlines and their passengers.

85

faster. By 1941 specifications like these were exciting the interest of the United States Air Force, which was looking for a new long-range aircraft, and detailed design work was put in hand. The problems of actually building such a radical plane proved immense, however, and it was July 1946 before the new Northrop XB55 flying wing actually took off. It was a remarkable aircraft, utterly original and a spectacular sight with its eight huge pusher propellers and wingspan of almost 55 metres (180 feet). Northrop soon replaced the propellers with jet engines and everyone agreed that the improved aircraft was a success, despite a fatal accident in its very last acceptance test. The pilot, Captain Glen Edwards, underestimated the rapidity with which the wing could pick up momentum in a dive and exceeded its maximum safe speed; the wings fell off, leaving the tiny centre section to plummet to earth with Edwards in it.

It was the post-war political climate rather than any problems with the aircraft that eventually led to the cancellation of the flying wing programme, and the concept of a long-range plane in which every portion of the body contributes lift remains attractive to many engineers to this day. One quite recent British Aerospace project envisaged a commercial version of the flying wing which would have boasted the greatest wingspan ever – about 100 metres – with passenger accommodation inside the wings. However, the company decided that customers were likely to be less than enthusiastic about the aircraft – there would have been a distinct lack of window seats – and evacuating them in an emergency would have been a real problem. The flying wing also proved to be a somewhat inflexible concept. While it is easy enough to lengthen or trim a conventional fuselage to accommodate the required number of passengers, the dynamics of a wing meant it was difficult to alter its size; and its prodigious span would have caused problems in most of the landing bays it was intended to occupy. In the end, for all the benefits of lift, the flying wing turned out to be an idea that is still awaiting acceptance from both airlines and passengers.

■ **WEIGHT AND SEA** The wings of a modern passenger liner do much more than provide lift, however; each is also packed with the fuel tanks that determine its range. Here the A3XX's size will for once act in its favour. Bigger wings mean greater fuel capacity and hence longer range. The longest routes operated today are 6700 nautical miles, and Airbus Industrie is promising that its new plane will be able to cross more than 7000 in a single hop. Later variants could have a range of up to 8000 nautical miles, enough to span the great width of the Pacific even against a head wind, and offer up to 25 per cent more fuel efficiency than existing aircraft – important, because the ratio of fuel consumed to passengers carried remains one of the key factors governing any airline's decision on which planes to buy.

Such efficiency can be achieved only if the loaded plane is kept as light as possible, and controlling the weight of the A3XX is perhaps the single most important key to its success. Each big bird will weigh 244 tons empty, and as much as 476 tons when fully loaded with passengers, luggage and fuel. Future 'stretched' versions could tip the scales at as much as 520 tons – if there were scales big enough to weigh them. This is not a problem when the plane is in the air, but taking off and landing are different matters.

Some of the largest aircraft ever built used the seas as their airfield. There, so long as the weather is relatively calm, there is no limit to the potential length of a big plane's runway. Flying boats and seaplanes – some of them big even by modern standards – were also the most obvious answer to the problems of long-distance and intercontinental flight in the days before the development of an international network of airports and landing fields.

Big flying boats were first developed during the First World War for reconnaissance and anti-submarine work. Some of the best designs came from a former Royal Navy lieutenant named John Porte, whose determination to maintain his links with the sea after he was invalided out of the service with tuberculosis resulted in the creation of a whole series of aircraft. The last and most impressive of these was the Felixstowe Fury (or Porte Super Baby, as it was affectionately known to its crews) of 1918, a five-engined triplane so big that it became the first aircraft to be fitted with power-assisted controls – an innovation that eventually led to modern fly-by-wire control systems.

The Felixstowe Fury was a very capable aircraft, able to fly at around 160 kilometres per hour and take off with a load of 15 tons. But not every flying boat of the period was so well designed, and some were quite freakish. By some way the most remarkable of all the projects in the years between the two world wars was the Italian Caproni Ca60 Triple-Hydro-Triplane, a plane that looked as clumsy as its name suggests. It was a nine-winged, eight-engined monstrosity once described as resembling 'a houseboat mating with a squadron of bombers'. Its designer, Count Caproni, had been successful during the First World War with a series of capable heavy bombers, and he knew all about the problems of power and wing area. But he did not, it seems, understand the need for stability and control. With the planned 100 passengers on board, the load on the Triple-Hydro-Triplane's nine wings would have had to be almost equally distributed to maintain stability, so any attempt to manoeuvre would potentially lead to disaster. In fact, the giant plane did manage one straight line flight of about 1600 metres over Lake Maggiore in the spring of 1921; the second time it took off, it struggled to a height of 18 metres then tilted its

'Like a houseboat mating with a squadron of bombers' – the outlandish Caproni Ca60 Triple-Hydro-Triplane had nine wings, eight engines and not a chance of inaugurating the transatlantic passenger service its Italian designer planned. On its second flight over Lake Maggiore, it rose briefly into the sky before plunging into the lake from a height of 18 metres.

nose down and dived straight into the lake – fortunately without killing its crew.

Caproni was forced to abandon his plans for a transatlantic, passenger-carrying air service, but later designers had more success. One of the last great flying boats, and still the largest aircraft ever built in Britain, was the Saunders-Roe Princess, the product of a small, specialized factory on the Isle of Wight. With the sea all around, Saunders-Roe was well placed to build giant flying boats and the Princess, which was intended to fly either to New York or across Africa and on towards the Far East and Australia, was designed to carry 105 passengers in some comfort. When the prototype was completed in 1951 it had ten propeller engines, a wingspan of 67 metres and a hull 45 metres long. It claimed several world records – biggest pressurized aircraft, biggest metal aircraft and even, with a speed of 580 kilometres per hour, fastest propeller-driven civil aircraft – but there were problems in finding the right engine, and although the prototype did fly it was becoming increasingly clear that the era of the flying boat was over. Not only were the planes costly to run – their boat-shaped hulls offered much greater air resistance than a conventional landplane – they were also often dangerous to operate and had an unenviable record of coming to grief while attempting to land in choppy seas. Furthermore, the large airports that were springing up around the world, generally close to major cities, rendered flying boats obsolescent.

Airports have, indeed, had to evolve as quickly as aircraft, and the advent of a plane as big as the A3XX is certain to force more changes on them. But Airbus Industrie cannot afford to be too radical. Modern runways are built to cope with a 747; currently the heaviest commercial aircraft in the world, it weighs perhaps 400 tons. The addition of an extra 120 tons of A3XX coming in to land could be enough to cause cracks and stress fractures that would be expensive and, more important, time-consuming to repair. Most airports will be reluctant to strengthen their runways to take the weight of bigger aircraft, so the solution is for the planes to have titanium-reinforced landing gear of unprecedented size, with twenty-four main wheels rather than a jumbo jet's sixteen to spread the load. To ensure that there is room for everything to fold away and be maintained, the wheels will be split between two gears conventionally mounted under the wings and two that will fold away into the fuselage itself.

Landing the aircraft is not the only problem that requires Airbus's engineers to consult closely with the airports that will play host to it. Huber is sure that his plane will be able to take off from existing runways, which tend to be around 3 kilometres long, but the size of the A3XX means that new terminals and new gates will often be required to accommodate an aircraft that fits in a box 80 metres square. If the new plane is too big for the facilities on the ground, no airline will want to buy it; it is simply impossible to shut down a busy airport for rebuilding work and any adaptations have to be fitted into lengthy renovation cycles. It can take thirty years to modernize an airport completely so Huber's big bird, a long-term project in itself, will have to become part of the forward plans of hundreds of airport managers across the globe.

Each and every one of these men and women will want to know about noise. Although today's passenger aircraft are far quieter than their predecessors, any really huge plane is likely to cause problems for people below. The Airbus team hopes to minimize one of the causes, air resistance on the landing gear and flaps, through careful design, but the main key is to reduce the plane's approach speed to a minimum. A 747 comes in to land at an upper speed of 154 knots; the A3XX is designed to make its final approach at 145 knots, a difference of 6 per cent which will nevertheless make the airliner a full 20 per cent quieter than its rival despite its greater bulk.

There is a final sting in the tail for a consortium that is hoping to sell airlines big birds to operate at busy airports. Although the new plane will certainly allow Airbus customers to maximize the potential of each of their valuable landing slots, it will be so big that it could cause problems for an aircraft coming in to land behind it. Any large plane churns the air through which it passes. Its wings slice along at hundreds of kilometres an hour and create a 'wake vortex' of miniature horizontal tornadoes that can be very dangerous if they strike a smaller aircraft following behind. Airliners coming in to land after a 747 are already forced to hang back almost 10 kilometres, and the simplest solution to the arrival of the new Airbus would be to leave an even longer gap between landing slots. However, if this cuts back too much on the number of slots actually available the advantage of loading hundreds more passengers into one aircraft would be wiped out. Failure to solve a single problem of this sort would render the whole multi-billion dollar A3XX project pointless.

With parking bays already filled to capacity at many of the world's airports, an aircraft as big as the A3XX poses practical problems for airlines: its size means that existing terminals will have to be adapted to accommodate it.

■ **THE GOLDEN GOOSE** Big as the A3XX is – and any plane that can dwarf a 747 is truly huge – it will not be the biggest aeroplane that has ever flown. Though there has not been an aircraft to match it since the dawn of the jet age, the Airbus giant is still overshadowed by a single monstrous flying boat that clawed its way briefly into the sky over Long Beach, California, on 2 November 1947, to set a series of records that still stand today.

The plane was the appropriately named H4 Hercules. Its wings spanned just under 100 metres (320 feet) – the length of a football field – and covered more than 1000 square metres (about 10 750 square feet), an area so big that two four-engined B–17 Flying Fortress bombers could have been parked underneath it without being visible from the air. Each wing was also more than 3 metres (9 feet) deep, easily high enough for the tallest of men to walk upright inside it. At the rear, a tailplane soared 24 metres (80 feet) into the air. The Hercules was not only broader than the A3XX with its suddenly puny span of 77 metres but also just over a metre taller. Admittedly, at 74 metres (240 feet) the flying boat was about 3 metres shorter than Huber's baby, but no fewer than eight large propeller engines had to be harnessed to haul it into the air and on to its designed cruising speed of 110 kilometres per hour; and its carrying capacity was enormous – 740 people, about 200 more than the earliest A3XXs will seat. Even more astonishingly, it was built almost wholly of wood and glue, an achievement that deserved more than the sarcastic press nickname 'Spruce Goose' by which it is still best known today.

The Spruce Goose was big, but it was big for a reason. Unlike the many freakish giants that have been built simply to awe, or to satisfy the vanity of their creators, the Hercules had a serious purpose. Conceived early in the United States' involvement in the Second World War, it was designed as a flying cargo ship that would outfox the U-boats preying on conventional shipping in the Atlantic sea lanes. Carrying capacity was paramount; the plane was built to ferry hundreds of fully equipped troops, 350 stretcher cases, 54 000 kilograms of supplies or a 60 ton Sherman tank safely from America to Europe. The enormous effort that was devoted to making it an efficient carrier of soldiers and cargo made it far more significant than previous monster aircraft, and one of the true precursors of all modern widebodied aircraft.

The great flying boat was the creation of two very different men. Both were enormously wealthy and both were patriots, but one was a single-minded business-man and the other an obsessive perfectionist, one of the greatest pilots of the age and also perhaps the most remarkable eccentric of the twentieth century. The businessman was Henry J. Kaiser, a noted industrialist and inventor of the liberty ship, a new type of cargo vessel built according to the principles of mass production rather than the painstaking crafts of the traditional shipyard. By the time Kaiser had his slipways running smoothly, he was building each liberty ship in only thirty days, a rate faster than that at which even Hitler's Wolf Packs could sink them. The airman was Howard Hughes, a remarkable polymath who, although famed latterly as a mad recluse, so obsessed by germs that he refused to step on a floor and was said to walk everywhere on toilet paper, enjoyed successful early careers as an oilman, aviator and film producer and turned an inheritance of $500 000 into a business empire worth billions of dollars.

The Hercules was Kaiser's idea, and he was able to use his considerable

Best known for the eccentricities he displayed towards the end of his long life, Howard Hughes deserves to be remembered as a brilliant aviator who held numerous world records before the Second World War. He designed and piloted the aircraft that he is shown captaining here – the H4 Hercules. It is still the largest aeroplane ever to fly.

gifts as a propagandist to get it heard in Washington. America's greatest aircraft manufacturers – including Douglas and Northrop, and Martin who built the B–10 and B–26 bombers – were sceptical. They doubted that a plane big enough to offer the desired cargo capacity could possibly fly. But the reaction was more favourable when Kaiser approached Hughes. Already the creator of a business empire to rival Kaiser's own, Hughes owned both TWA, one of America's largest airlines, and the Hughes Aircraft Company, an establishment he had set up to build the specialist racing planes with which he had personally captured records for speed over a measured mile, for the fastest time between Los Angeles and New York and, finally, for an aerial circumnavigation of the globe when he smashed the old record of one

The Hercules' solitary flight failed to prove whether it could possibly have done what its designer claimed for it. But it did confound the many critics who had accused Hughes of wasting government funds on a machine that would never fly.

week and nineteen hours by exactly four days. Under his management the company had capitalized on its unusual background to become one of the leading designers of specialist aircraft in the world, and the giant flying boat was exactly the sort of project to excite his interest.

Hughes decided immediately that he would have to take full control of the practicalities of the project. Kaiser had no knowledge of aeronautics and indeed had come to their meeting with little more than some artists' impressions and a vague conception of the sort of dimensions his flying boat would need; he soon became less important to the project, and eventually resigned from it completely. But for Hughes, it became an obsession. Caught up at the time with his career in the film industry – he had recently discovered an actress named Jane Russell and was busy producing her controversial movie debut *The Outlaw* – he spent his days on the lot and his evenings sketching a series of giant aircraft. He considered planes with twin hulls and anything from four to eight engines before settling on a massive single-hull design. The idea was to build a fleet of 5000 of these flying boats, and in November 1942 Kaiser-Hughes secured a contract for two prototypes and a stationary test-bed from the United States government, who agreed to pay a total of $18 million. One prototype was to be ready and tested in just ten months.

It soon became clear that the details of the contract meant little to Hughes. Whatever the needs of the Allies and their merchant marine, he was going to take his time and ensure that the design of his boat was as nearly perfect as possible; the ten months passed and there was little to show for the government's investment other than a wind tunnel test model and one of the most prodigious orders ever placed in California for birch veneer: 47 000 metres (29 miles) of it.

By the time the design was finally completed to Hughes' satisfaction $12.5 million of government money had been spent on the single prototype, it was June 1946, the war was over and the whole project had recently been declared surplus to national requirements and made the subject of a Congressional investigation into the misuse of government funds.

Other men might have written off the flying boat at this point, but Hughes' personal pride demanded that it be finished, at his own expense, if only to prove to his many critics that the Hercules would actually fly. He spent another year and anything up to $22 million on the project, refining his plans and testing. Gradually the giant sections, some more than 60 metres (200 feet) long and others weighing up to 55 tons, were assembled in a purpose-built dry dock. While this was happening, Hughes built a mechanical simulator and began to practise flying the largest aircraft ever built.

The Hercules would be far from easy to fly. The distances between the cockpit and the control surfaces were unprecedentedly vast, and the flaps and rudders themselves so big that it would have taken the strength of 200 men to operate them without mechanical help. For these reasons, Hughes and his team had designed an untested hydraulic control system. They also added more than 50 kilometres (30 miles) of electric wiring and twenty-eight intercom stations which were scattered throughout the gigantic interior so that members of the crew could report unforeseen problems in time for the pilot to react to them. Of the eighteen crew selected for the preliminary trials, fifteen were mechanics or engineers.

The huge flying boat was finally floated out on to the waters of Long Beach Sound and on 2 November 1947 Hughes boarded his aircraft. He revved each of his eight Pratt & Whitney engines in turn and began to taxi out along the 4.8 kilometre test course. There were waves out in the sound and the noise inside the Hercules rose as its speed reached around 65 kilometres per hour. The plane seemed to be handling well, and Hughes made the return journey at almost 150 kilometres per hour. As the speed rose, the noise inside the wooden hull fell; the Spruce Goose was skimming the waves rather than forcing its way through them. Hughes then turned the aircraft again to begin a third test run.

Once again the engines screamed, louder now as Hughes applied more throttle. He called for 15 degrees of flap, the first sure sign he intended to fly. As the plane pushed past the 150 kilometre per hour barrier there were what looked like explosions, one from each engine; they were actually balls of vapour springing from the propellers as they chewed at the air at full speed. Then, suddenly, the Hercules was airborne; the largest plane in the world, doing what it had been engineered to do, flying with surprising grace about 10 metres above the waves.

The flight did not last long. The plane was airborne for only a minute, and flew perhaps $1\frac{1}{2}$ kilometres before Hughes set it down again, relieved perhaps to have proved his point without recklessly endangering his passengers. He taxied back to the flying boat's dock and shut down the engines.

The Spruce Goose never flew again. Hughes wanted it to and spent heavily on new engines and further modifications. But he would never allow anyone else to pilot his creation and, as time passed, he became more and more caught up in other parts of his business and then progressively more withdrawn and solitary. In 1953 floods badly damaged the plane and, although it was repaired, it was by then obsolete and there was never any real chance that tests would be resumed. Hughes preserved his aircraft and after his death in 1976 it was eventually turned into a museum piece. It still exists, though it has now been dismantled and sits, waiting for a new home to be built around it, on a hillside above Portland, Oregon: the plane that missed the boat.

It is impossible, on such slender evidence, to judge the true capabilities of Howard Hughes' Hercules. Nevertheless, its brief flight showed that giant planes could handle well if they were carefully designed, and its wide body (8.5 metres/28 feet, nearly 2 metres wider than that of the A3XX) and enormous theoretical passenger capacity emboldened future aircraft designers.

■ **A WORLD IN FLIGHT** On the one hand, Jean-Jacques Huber can draw inspiration from Howard Hughes and his Hercules. Their short hop proved, if proof were needed, that an aircraft as big as the A3XX can actually fly. On the other, he knows that his plane could share the fate of the Spruce Goose: it could prove itself viable only to be written off by forces beyond his control. Some critics are surprised that the whole project has not been cancelled already, and there will be other crises before the A3XX even takes to the air.

What keeps the Airbus Industrie team going is faith in figures – not just the complex engineering calculations that prove their big bird will fly but also the statistics that point inexorably to the need for yet larger planes. Around the globe, passenger air traffic continues to increase by 5 per cent per year, which means that the number of people flying is likely to double in fifteen years and triple within twenty-three. At that rate, logic suggests, at some point towards the end of the twenty-first century the whole population of the world will be airborne simultaneously. Huber fully intends that the majority of them will be flying Airbus Industrie planes.

CHAPTER FOUR

TALL

P hilippe Petit breathed deeply and stepped off the parapet into space. Holding his heavy balancing pole carefully at waist level, he placed first one foot and then the other on the taut, thin wire he had stretched at roof level between the twin towers of the World Trade Centre – the mightiest buildings in New York, city of skyscrapers. The space he had to cross was tiny, less than 30 metres, and Petit had walked that distance on the high wire a thousand times before and survived. But he had no safety net, no harness; a slip, a fierce gust of wind – or simply a movement of the towers, which sway from side to side by up to a metre at that great height – could pitch him off and send him flailing down the 150 storeys to the ground.

Almost half a kilometre below, in the concrete chasm beneath his feet, the first early morning passer-by glanced upward and noticed the small black-clad figure apparently suspended in mid-air. Soon a large crowd of office workers had gathered and watched in horrified fascination as Petit walked for an hour from one tower to the other. Occasionally he varied his act by pausing to lie flat on his wire.

Long before the French tightrope walker was ready to come down police officers and the centre's patrolmen had arrived to end the stunt and begin an investigation into how Petit had evaded security to reconnoitre the centre, carry all the necessary equipment up to the roof, hide there overnight and, in the dawn's early light, use a crossbow to fire 40 metres of steel wire from the roof of one tower to an accomplice waiting on its twin. For several minutes the police argued with Petit while he balanced just out of reach. At last he agreed to give himself up and stepped back on to the roof. He was seized, handcuffed and escorted to a psychiatric ward, where he was placed under observation.

Petit's tightrope walk was hardly the act of a madman. It was painstakingly planned and its timing – it took place in August 1974, less than a year after the trade centre opened – was calculated to generate publicity for his act. But the Frenchman was not interested simply in press coverage. He saw himself as an artist and the vast scale of the buildings as a challenge. Although he had performed similar stunts before – between the towers of the cathedral of Notre Dame in Paris in 1971 and above the Sydney Harbour Bridge in 1973 – the World Trade Centre had a very special quality that transcended the banality of its glass-box architecture. It

**Previous page:
Workers defy
gravity during the
construction of a
skyscraper.**

was more than just a very tall building. It was a skyscraper: the religious symbol of an agnostic century, man's monument to man.

■ **RISING IN THE EAST** For sixty-five years the tallest building in the world has been American. Its site may have been sometimes in New York and sometimes in Chicago, but the record has been held by the United States ever since the astonishing art deco Chrysler Building surpassed the Eiffel Tower and topped out at 319 metres (1046 feet) in August 1930.

In 1996, however, the Petronas Towers will open and the honour will pass to the Malaysian capital, Kuala Lumpur. These twin skyscrapers, which will be linked by a bridge a third of the way up their sheer walls, are 460 metres high and surpass the Sears Tower in Chicago – the tallest building in the world for the last two decades – by 17 metres. They are designed by Cesar Pelli & Associates, who built Britain's highest tower at Canary Wharf in London, and are so big that for the people living and working at their summit the ground will be a distant memory. Indeed, in order to make the buildings workable and lend them any sense of human scale, the architects have been forced to include not one but several atriums scattered throughout the towers to divide them into more manageable spaces.

The Petronas Towers are only the first of five huge building projects that mark the re-emergence of the Far East as the world's dominant economy. Hong Kong's 468 metre Nina Tower is scheduled for completion in 1997, the year the British crown colony will be returned to the People's Republic of China. China's burgeoning financial might will pay for two large skyscrapers in Shanghai, and an even mightier one in Chonquing where the authorities stipulated a building of at least 100 storeys. What they will get is a 516 metre tower with an eight-storey high entrance hall and a luxury hotel at its top.

The largest project is planned by Japan. It is an 860 metre high monolith called the Millennium Tower, the most ambitious building yet conceived by even that ambitious power. The sheer scale of this self-contained city in which up to 50 000 people will live and work is staggering. The tower will be conical with a 130 metre diameter base, and 188 storeys high. It will easily dwarf every other skyscraper ever built – and exceed almost all the limits known to the architects and engineers of giant buildings.

The 460 metre Petronas Towers in Malaysia; currently under construction (above right) they will be the tallest buildings in the world when they are completed in 1996 – the first time since 1930 that the record has been held outside the United States.

The Millennium Tower will have to resist lateral wind pressures four times as strong as any yet encountered by a skyscraper – and because it will rise in the centre of an earthquake zone it must be proof against tremors. The people within it will have to be offered a comfortable working environment and conveyed up and down its dizzying height at speed. They must also be safeguarded against fire. Not the least significant problem will be raising finance. The project's originator, the giant Obayashi Corporation, has yet to find a city with pockets deep enough to pay for it. The tower will not necessarily be built in Japan and, indeed, Shanghai is one possible location although the building's sponsors have done little other than carry out a preliminary survey. Potential backers are perhaps right to be hesitant. For all its tremendous sophistication, the tower could be little more than a short-lived wonder, destined to be surpassed within a decade or two by an even mightier building. And, however strong and well constructed it is, it will have only the slenderest chance of enduring as long as the first tall monument built by man.

■ **FIRST WONDER** For more than 4400 years – nine-tenths of recorded history – the greatest and tallest man-made structure in the world was the Great Pyramid of Khufu (or Cheops), ruler of Fourth Dynasty Egypt. Although its precise purpose remains obscure – a sarcophagus stands in the King's Chamber but there is no evidence that it ever held the pharaoh's mummy – there is no denying the pyramid's enormity nor its remarkable sophistication. Its builders aligned its sides to the four cardinal points of the compass – probably with the help of observations of the sun and stars – and each is almost exactly 230 metres long; the difference between the longest and the shortest sides is no more than 20 centimetres, an error of one in 1134. The pyramid rises almost 150 metres above the desert at Giza west of Cairo and encloses an area large enough to contain St Peter's in Rome, St Paul's and Westminster Abbey in London and the cathedrals of Milan and Florence. It was built, apparently entirely by hand, of separate limestone blocks some of which weighed as much as 15 tons. Their average weight was 2.5 tons – 6.5 million tons of rock in all.

The pyramid's sheer bulk is all the more remarkable when the paucity of resources available to its builder, Khufu's cousin Hemon, is taken into account. Although there was certainly no shortage of labour – most of Egypt's great monuments were probably built by peasant workers conscripted while the Nile was in flood and the fields inundated – nor of suitable stone, the ancient Egyptians did not use pulleys or blocks and tackle and their chief building aids were rollers and levers.

According to the ancient Greek historian Herodotus, the Great Pyramid was built as a series of terraces; blocks of stone were hauled up all four sides simultaneously with 'machines made of short timbers' – probably some form of lever – and the structure was then filled out and faced with blocks of gleaming white limestone from a quarry east of Cairo to create a smooth and regular surface. Herodotus' theory has been challenged many times. Other suggestions are that the blocks may have been hauled on wooden rollers up an enormous ramp which stretched out into the desert and was continually raised and lengthened as construction progressed, or that they were pushed up a similar structure that wound its way up the outside of the pyramid in a spiral. Such methods would have involved an enormous amount of labour, however, and a few years ago a master-builder named Peter Hodges successfully demonstrated that it was indeed possible to hoist stones the size of the pyramid's blocks using timber levers, each with a metal-shod 'foot' that protruded at right angles from one end.

The pyramid builders' first task was to level their chosen site on the west bank of the Nile. They probably achieved this by adapting irrigation methods used along the river's banks. A low mud wall would have been built around the space to be levelled and a series of trenches dug across the area. Water would then have been diverted from the river to flood the enclosure. By measuring down from its horizontal surface a constant depth could be established in the channels and when the water was drained away all the foundations could be excavated to the same level.

The logistics of cutting and transporting the huge limestone blocks would have been more complicated. The quarrymen probably used hard rocks and copper saws and chisels to carve out the softer stone, then drove wooden wedges into holes cut into the bottom of each block and wetted them. Water caused the wedges to expand so that the limestone cracked and the blocks were freed. The stone was transported down the river by barge and hauled to the pyramid by sledge and muscle-power.

The Egyptians used simple surveying instruments and are known to have employed plumb lines and set squares; with their help, it would certainly have been possible to place the stones accurately. Mortar was probably smeared over at least two surfaces to act as a lubricant and the stone dragged into its final position with ropes, or pushed there with levers. The workmanship was such that a postcard cannot be inserted into the space between the blocks on the outside of the pyramid.

Although it is known that the Great Pyramid was constructed around a central core of natural rock that stood in the centre of the site on which it was built, its internal structure remains a matter of guesswork. But if Hemon followed the pattern established by Imhotep, the semi-legendary Egyptian architect and engineer who first conceived building in stone, he would have first constructed a series of buttresses around the core, each leaning in at an angle of about 75 degrees. Further layers of buttresses, slightly shorter than their predecessors, would then have been added around the outside of the inner series, eventually producing a step pyramid to which outer casing stones could be added. These casing stones were also inclined slightly inwards to increase the stability of the structure.

The immensity of the Great Pyramid has never been excelled, but tall buildings were not unknown elsewhere in the ancient world. The Pharos Tower of Alexandria, built by Sostratus Cnidus in 270 BC to act as a lighthouse for ships approaching the port, is thought to have been more than 100 metres high. This wonder of the ancient world stood for one and a half millennia before it was destroyed by an earthquake in the fourteenth century. Made of marble, it was built in three sections: the lowest one was square, the middle one octagonal and the highest portion circular. The fire that burnt continuously at its top was magnified by a large mirror and was visible up to 50 kilometres out to sea.

The Pharos Tower, like the pyramids, was not built to be lived in and, in general, the ancients experienced few of the problems of overcrowding that lent impetus to the construction of skyscrapers in our own century. Rome, however, was an exception. By the fourth century BC the city had so many inhabitants that the first true apartment buildings were constructed to ease the growing pressure on space. The architect Vitruvius, writing in the first century BC, described problems that would be familiar to the men who pushed New York and Chicago skywards: 'In view of the unlimited number of citizens, it is necessary to provide dwellings without number. Therefore ... necessity has driven the Romans to build high. By the use of stone piers, crowning courses of burnt brick and concrete walls, high buildings are raised with several storeys, producing highly convenient apartments.'

The fragmentary evidence that has survived suggests that some Roman buildings were at least seven storeys high, although after the disastrous fire of 64 AD the emperor Nero issued a decree that limited new blocks to a height of no more than 21 metres, or up to six storeys.

Although these apartment blocks were big for their day, they were dwarfed by religious monuments. It was a trend that continued into the Christian era, when a city's largest building was almost invariably a cathedral whose towers were visible from miles away. Even in the late nineteenth century the monument to George Washington in Washington, DC, the world's tallest structure when it was erected, was an exception. In Paris the towers of Notre Dame remained the capital's most noted sight – until a little-known engineer named Gustave Eiffel suggested marking the centenary in 1889 of the French Revolution by erecting an iron tower twice as tall as the Great Pyramid, from which Parisians could gaze down upon their city from an unprecedented height.

■ **'METAL ASPARAGUS'** For a building that came to symbolize a nation – and one that was an engineering triumph to boot – the Eiffel Tower had an inauspicious birth. It was intended to stand for only a little longer than the event it commemorated, and designed to be no more than a spectacular look-out point and a symbol of France's growing industrial might.

The tower was without doubt the largest iron structure yet built, a 300 metre tall jigsaw put together from 15 000 parts. It was also constructed with remarkable sureness and rapidity. It had taken perhaps twenty years and the labour of 100 000 men to build the Great Pyramid, but the Eiffel Tower was erected, without accident and practically without trial or experiment, by a workforce of only 250 in little more than a year.

The main reason for this efficiency was Eiffel. Although he had become a structural engineer and an ironmaster only by accident – his early ambition to work in an uncle's vinegar factory was thwarted by a family quarrel – he successfully built up one of France's leading ironworks and became an expert in the properties of metals and the design of bridges. It was Eiffel who first measured the action of the wind against tall bridges, and stiffened them with trusses; and it was he who built the metal skeleton for the Statue of Liberty, France's gift to the United States

to commemorate the alliance between the two countries during the American Revolution.

Eiffel's detailed knowledge of wind and iron was invaluable when he designed the monument that bears his name. Theoretical calculations soon satisfied him that the best possible design was a deceptively fragile-looking lattice of iron girders, strong enough to support its own weight but too sparsely built for wind pressure to become a threat. Although the tower occupies a substantial plot 1.6 hectares in area, it is so light that if it were compressed into a single sheet the size of its base it would be less than 7 centimetres thick. Nevertheless, it is strong enough to resist

No building has been the world's tallest for longer than the Great Pyramid. It was built in c.2500 BC from 6½ million tons of rock fitted together with impressive precision by tens of thousands of peasant conscripts.

fiercer winds than have ever been experienced in the French capital – it will stand firm in steady gusts of more than 215 kilometres per hour.

Once he was satisfied that his creation would be safe, Eiffel had to meet the challenge of designing its bewilderingly complex maze of latticework. He decided to base the tower on four large iron buttresses that lean inwards at 54 degrees – almost identical in inclination to the slope of the Great Pyramid – and rest on the solid concrete pylons of the foundations. They form the structure's 'legs' and are cross-braced diagonally, horizontally and vertically throughout their journey to the tower's massive first platform. Although they also appear to be supported by iron arches that curve from one buttress to its neighbour these are purely decorative and represent Eiffel's attempt to placate the outraged criticisms of the Parisian literati, who united in their condemnation of his outlandish new construction of 'metal asparagus'. After the first platform the structure becomes more slender and elegant, curving towards the vertical so that its four great columns meet. There is a second platform and, higher still above the city, an observation deck and a mast. Elevators run inside the buttresses to preserve the integrity of the structure; making them work on such an incline was a challenge in itself.

A number of fundamental engineering problems had to be solved during the construction of the Eiffel Tower. The most difficult was to ensure that the buttresses leant in at precisely the correct angle so that the first platform, 55 metres above the ground, could be positioned correctly. If the angle of inclination had been out by as little as a tenth of one degree, the rivet holes that were to secure the platform to the buttresses would have been 127 millimetres out of alignment and the rivets could not have been fixed. Eiffel's solution to this problem was typically ingenious. He devised temporary wooden supports that pressed against the tower's 'legs' at ground level and held them at the correct angle. Each support was mounted on hydraulic jacks so that if the buttresses were too low for the platform they could be lifted by tiny increments until the rivet holes were perfectly aligned. At that point rivets would be hammered in to secure the platform while slender iron wedges were rammed into the newly opened gap between the tower's 'feet' and the concrete pylons on which they stood. Eiffel also installed large steel cylinders filled with fine sand alongside the wooden supports. Plungers pressed against the legs were slotted into the cylinders and if the buttresses proved to be slightly too high a whole gigantic

The Eiffel Tower was one of the most efficiently constructed structures ever built. Fewer than 250 workmen erected it in little more than a year, and brought it in under budget and in time for the 1889 celebrations of the French Revolution.

iron column could be gradually lowered simply by allowing sand to trickle from the bottom of the cylinder.

Once the first platform was firmly in place, construction work on the remainder of the tower could proceed apace. Eiffel and his mechanical engineers installed a series of 'creeping cranes' which could be moved upwards on the rails that were being installed for the elevator system. Because the weight of any single component was limited to no more than 3 tons, the speed of the building work was kept high. The tower was completed within Eiffel's schedule and cost 5 per cent less than his original estimate. It opened in time for the Great Exhibition held in Paris in 1889 and proved immensely popular. More than two million people visited it during its first year and, when the twenty years it had been allotted by the organizers of the centennial were up and it faced demolition, it was saved by the interest of wireless companies who saw its potential as a radio mast.

■ **SKELETONS OF STEEL** For nearly fifty years, the Eiffel Tower remained the tallest man-made structure in the world. Even in the United States, where sky-scrapers had begun to reach ever higher, there was nothing to match it in sheer height until the 1930s. But although its shape and purpose had little in common with the towers and apartment blocks of the New World, Gustave Eiffel's masterpiece shared one important feature with every tall building that has followed it: a metal skeleton.

The iron or steel frame – surely the single most important development in the history of tall buildings since Hemon's workers laid down their tools – first appeared in its complete form in the United States at about the time Eiffel was conceiving his tower, but architects and engineers had been groping towards the invention for many years. Prefabricated cast-iron façades had been introduced in the middle of the nineteenth century, and bridge-builders had been demonstrating the usefulness of metal frames for many years before that. Nevertheless, the first structure to feature a fully worked-out internal metal frame was the ten-storey Home Insurance Building erected in Chicago between 1883 and 1885.

It was an unremarkable piece of architecture, but an important piece of engineering. Its builder, William LeBaron Jenney, recognized that a steel framework could endow his structure with remarkable properties. A lattice of vertical and horizontal steel beams could bear the weight and stresses of a tall building far more efficiently than masonry walls, which would need to be prohibitively heavy to support both the weight of multiple storeys above them and the pressure of wind pushing against them. Buildings that had hitherto been limited to no more than a dozen or so floors could thus be extended upwards almost indefinitely and still be stronger than their masonry forebears.

The construction of a steel-framed skyscraper begins with the excavation of its foundations. Sometimes – particularly in a city such as New York which is built on granite – these are enough to support a completed tower. But it is more usual for the foundations themselves to be supplemented by steel or reinforced concrete piles strong enough to bear the enormous weight that is about to be placed on them.

When the foundations have been dug, concrete is poured into them to support the first of the steel girders that will form the frame and the tower begins to rise. Girders are secured to the concrete with high-strength bolts and the columns are connected to the main beams which will support the various floors. Once the first three or four storeys have been completed in skeleton, steel floor-plates or reinforced concrete slabs are laid across filler beams with the help of small cranes which slowly ascend the outside of the skyscraper as it grows, much as those on the Eiffel Tower did. The most modern building methods involve fast-tracking the construction process – much of the material that will be needed is fabricated in bulk and construction of the lower storeys starts even before the design of the upper reaches of the building has been completed. An experienced construction gang with its hoisters and burners, welders, plumbers-up, safety-men and connectors, can erect a skyscraper at the rate of a floor every three or four days; and the process is broadly similar whether it is a steel-framed structure or one in reinforced concrete.

The architects and engineers working on the project are meanwhile fully employed in calculating the manifold stresses and strains their new building will have to resist if it is to stay upright. The sheer weight of the tower is the first consideration. While its top floor need bear no more than the roof, the one beneath it must support twice as much weight – its own and that of the upper one – and so on, down to the ground floor, which may easily have 100 storeys of steel, wood and concrete plus office equipment bearing down on it. Wind is also a major problem, particularly in the tallest structures, because the forces to be resisted increase with the square of the skyscraper's height. The building must be rigid enough to remain upright in a gale and its tendency to sway must be kept within limits that its inhabitants find bearable.

For most of this century, the twin hazards of weight and wind were dealt with separately. Rather than being used to create a protective outer skeleton, load-bearing girders were concentrated in a stiff inner core of steel, which protected the lift shafts and main service ducts and pipes. This was surrounded by a much more flexible external frame designed to tackle wind pressure. Because the weight bearing downwards on the main girders was far greater than the pressure from the wind, it was unnecessary for the external frame to be unwieldy. An additional advantage was that the inner core could be considerably strengthened by cross-bracing; this is not possible on an external frame because steel diagonals severely impede the placement of windows.

In the last two decades, refinements of the older system have been introduced in a number of structures, including New York's World Trade Centre and the John Hancock Building and record-breaking Sears Tower in Chicago. The engineers of each of these buildings found a way to transfer load-bearing to the outer skeleton and do away with the central steel core which they replaced with a far lighter concrete one. The ninety-five storey John Hancock Building, for example, adopted huge external diagonal bracings which obscured the view through one window in three and, in the opinion of one architectural critic, turned the tower into 'a looming giant, a great cowboy stalking the town' – but also cut steel construction costs by 42 per cent. The World Trade Centre has no diagonals, but the columns that make up its external structure are only one metre apart. This provides strength but means that there are no large windows in the towers. The 443 metre (1454 ft) Sears Tower took the new concept of 'tube buildings'

The Sears Tower in Chicago, currently the world's tallest building, was one of the first skyscrapers to be built around a concrete core.

to its limit by bundling together no fewer than nine steel-framed tubes, each 523 square metres (5630 square feet) in area. Architecturally, the result is an interesting structure in which the tubes rise together for the first third of their journey after which they terminate at different heights. Only two of the tubes soar all the way to the top of the tower. To its engineer, Fazlur Kahn, however, the chief triumph of the design is the weight it saves. The Sears Tower is 22 per cent lighter per square metre than the Empire State Building with its central core.

■ **GOING UP** Steel frame construction was only one of two essential inventions that made modern skyscrapers possible. The other was an efficient method of conveying the progressively greater numbers of people who lived and worked in these buildings from street level to their offices and homes. The solution was that safest of all forms of mass transportation: the lift.

In the United States alone, passenger elevators travel the equivalent of more than three billion kilometres a year with only about a thousand accidents and scarcely a fatality between them. In 1980, one major manufacturer claimed that its lifts carried the equivalent of the population of the world every nine days. Few elements in a skyscraper are less ostentatious or easier to ignore, but imagine labouring on foot to the top of any major building and the vital importance of safe, swift and efficient lifts is readily apparent.

The most basic form of elevator – a wooden platform raised and lowered by ropes and a winch – was a simple enough invention. Vitruvius described such contraptions in the first century BC, and even then the idea seems to have been more than two centuries old. But for the next 2000 years lifts were generally regarded as being dangerously unsafe: a frayed hemp rope or an overloaded platform was all it took to cause disaster. Steam lifts, which first appeared in Britain in about 1800, did little to improve matters. They were used solely to carry freight.

It became clear that the key to making a passenger-carrying elevator lay not in developing the winding and hoisting mechanism but in perfecting reliable safety equipment. The problem was not solved until the 1850s, when an American inventor named Elisha Graves Otis had the idea of fitting spring-loaded clamps below the car which would act as a brake by automatically gripping the lift's guide-rails if the hoist rope snapped. Otis patented his invention in 1853 and gave the first public demonstration of its significance in the most dramatic possible fashion at New York's Crystal Palace Exposition that same year. The prototype Otis lift was fitted within an iron skeleton of a shaft so that the public had a clear view as the car, with its inventor in it, was hoisted above their heads. Then Otis called out for the cables to be cut and the crowd held its breath, half expecting the lift to plunge to the ground. But the safety clamps did their job and Otis called down to the throng: 'All safe, gentlemen.'

Otis' demonstration changed the face of urban architecture. Steel had made the skyscraper possible, but the lift made it practicable. Within a few years buildings began to reach further towards the sky than had seemed possible when upper storeys had to be reached by foot and anything with more than five floors was regarded as impractical. By the end of the nineteenth century ten- or even fifteen-storey blocks were being efficiently served by elevators that achieved the hitherto unrealized distinction of making upper floors as desirable, if not more so, as those closer to the ground. The first working Otis lift was installed in New York's five-storey E. V. Haughtwout & Co. department store in 1857. It was powered by steam and took one minute to ascend the floors. Contemporaries regarded this as astonishingly swift, but at that speed it would take twenty minutes to reach the top of a large modern skyscraper.

There were still plenty of dead ends to explore. A car installed in the Fifth Avenue Hotel, New York, in 1859 was raised by a large vertical screw rather than with ropes. But on the whole, progress was rapid. Hydraulic lifts were introduced, and the first electrically powered elevator, raised by a winding drum installed in the basement, appeared in the Demarest Building in New York in 1889. Electricity proved to be cheaper than steam or hydraulic power, and the machinery it required took up much less space. Another, even more important, advantage was that an electrically powered lift could ascend at a constant speed rather than at one that was dependent upon the load in the passenger car. The elevator remained crude in other respects, however. Hand ropes, linked directly to electric switches, were used as controls until push-button panels made their appearance in 1894. By 1920 a small but significant further advance was made with the introduction of call buttons which allowed waiting passengers to summon the lift. This invention did away with the need for an attendant and maximized the efficiency of elevators that had

The invention of the lift to convey passengers to and from their homes and workplaces was an essential step towards making tall buildings possible. Today high-speed lifts in skyscrapers can travel at up to 500 metres a minute.

previously had to stop at every floor on the chance that someone might be waiting.

A number of limits still had to be overcome. Winding drums, which gathered up cable as the lift rose or fell, could not work safely at speeds in excess of 120 metres per minute, and there were a number of accidents when automatic cut-off switches failed and a lift being hauled upwards by a drum installed at the top of its shaft crashed into the winding gear and destroyed it. The solution to this problem was the traction drive. Invented in Britain in 1895, this substituted a continuous loop of cable for the single hoist. With the passenger car on one side of the loop and a counterweight on the other which rose as the lift descended and fell as it rose again, the traction drive enabled lift engineers to overcome the speed limits of the winding drum.

It was also easier to install than the old-fashioned winding mechanism, cheaper to use and significantly safer. Indeed, safety could almost be guaranteed because it was possible to fix the length of the cable loop relative to the height of the lift shaft in such a way that the counterweight reached the bottom of the shaft before the car could rise high enough to collide with the overhead driving drum.

With the problems of power and safety largely solved by the turn of the century, the main barriers to the construction of excessively tall buildings were the number of passengers an elevator could carry and the speed at which it could rise. The continual introduction of more powerful machinery soon improved the latter. In 1931 the lifts installed in the Empire State Building travelled at 365 metres (1197 feet) per minute, and the express elevators fitted in the John Hancock Building in Chicago four decades later ascended at almost 550 metres (1800 feet) per minute. By the time the Sears Tower was constructed, fast lifts were reaching more than 30 kilometres (18 miles) per hour, swift enough to take visitors to the top of the 103-storey building in less than a minute. Such speeds are still a far cry from those

The Flat Iron Building on Broadway is one of the earliest of New York's skyscrapers, and still one of the most arresting. It proved a paradise for voyeurs who gathered to watch its downdraughts whip up the skirts of female passers-by.

achieved by the world's fastest elevators, the ear-popping 65 kilometres (40 miles) per hour winding cages that take workers into the bowels of South Africa's 2 kilometre deep mine shafts, but they still come at the expense of a slightly uncomfortable pit-of-the-stomach lurch as the ride begins. The emphasis on speed seems more typical of Western buildings than the skyscrapers of the Far East, where a higher premium is placed on comfort.

Passenger capacity proved a trickier problem to solve than sheer speed. An enormous number of people work in the tallest office blocks, and the delays while a lift stops at almost every floor to allow passengers to embark or disembark can be interminable. The simplest solution was to introduce more and more lifts and shafts, but this significantly reduced the amount of usable space within a skyscraper and also imposed severe restrictions on its architects. A more sophisticated answer to the problem, perfected in the World Trade Centre, was to mix high-speed express elevators with banks of slower lifts that travel only part of the distance up and down. The trade centre has two huge 'sky lobbies' on its forty-fourth and seventy-eighth storeys, reached by eleven vast express lifts that stop only at these key floors. Passengers for the forty or so lower floors travel in one of twenty-four slower local cars, while those going to the higher levels take an express elevator to the appropriate sky lobby and then transfer to similar banks of lifts that shuttle between floors forty-four and seventy-seven and seventy-eight and 110.

■ **THE EMPIRE STATE** In the early twentieth century the steel frame and the passenger lift were put to practical use in a succession of increasingly gigantic skyscrapers that sprouted in brick and concrete from the soils of Chicago and of New York, capital in all but name of what George Washington called the 'empire state'. In 1903 New York built the much-loved Flatiron Building, a wedge-shaped 87 metre (285 foot) office block of remarkable beauty which dominated a triangular site on Broadway. At its apex the wedge is only 2 metres (6 feet) across which gives the building a sheer and slender appearance when viewed head-on. The Flatiron was also famous for its downdraughts, which whipped up the petticoats of female passers-by and added a semi-permanent population of gawking men to the sightseers who came to marvel at it. Its height was soon exceeded by that of the 110 metre (360 foot) Singer Building of 1908, and its area by the gigantic twin thirty-nine-storey blocks of the Equitable Life Assurance Building. The latter was completed in 1913, just before the introduction of zoning laws, and added more than 110 000 square metres (over a million square feet) of rentable office space to the city's total.

However, the most successful and beloved of all New York's early skyscrapers was the Woolworth Building of 1913. Designed by the *beaux-arts* architect Cass Gilbert, it combined a bulky main structure with a large but elegant Gothic tower which was set back twice during its ascent and topped, at 242 metres (794 feet), with an ornate crown. As well as providing space for 14 000 workers and enough power to light a city of 50 000, the building is probably the largest ever built that has never known a mortgage. Frank Woolworth's stores were so successful that he was able to pay the $13 million construction cost in cash. It was a worthwhile investment; the skyscraper remains the company's headquarters to this day.

The Woolworth Building with its fifty-five storeys and 5000 windows remained the highest building in New York – and the tallest inhabited structure in the world – for eighteen years. Two skyscrapers locked in mortal combat beat it: the Bank of Manhattan Company Building of H. Craig Severance, and the Chrysler Building designed by Severance's one-time partner William Van Alen. Naked lust for sheer height was spectacularly manifested during the construction of these towers. When Van Alen announced his building would be 282 metres (925 feet) tall, and therefore bigger than the Manhattan Company's, Severance added a flag-pole to his tower to take it 60 centimetres (24 inches) above the Chrysler's planned height. Van Alen countered by secretly assembling a 37 metre (121 foot) spire he called the 'vertex' inside the crown of his building. Once Severance's tower had topped out and there was no chance of adding to it, Van Alen's vertex was hoisted out through a specially prepared hatch in the roof of his tower. The Chrysler's right to the title of the tallest building in the world had been decisively asserted.

It was a spectacular but empty gesture. Another building was already rising in central Manhattan, one that was destined to define the skyscraper for decades to come. The Empire State Building on Fifth Avenue was New York's real answer to the Eiffel Tower, a structure that combined elegance with extreme height and became a symbol of the city it graced. The building was ordered by a businessman named John Jacob Raskob and his specifications determined much of the basic design decided on by the architects Shreve, Lamb and Harmon. Raskob wanted a

The art deco tip of the Chrysler Building in New York is topped by a spire that was constructed secretly inside the roof by its architect, William Van Alen, to make it taller than its rival, the Bank of Manhattan Company Building.

The beloved symbol of New York, the Empire State Building was erected in only eight months. It proved its strength by surviving a collision with a United States Air Force bomber which tore into its seventy-ninth floor on 28 July 1945, killing more than a dozen people but leaving the building with the equivalent of little more than a scratch.

million cubic metres (more than 35 million cubic feet) of space squeezed into a lot only 60 by 130 metres (197 by 426 feet), and he wanted the building open by 1 May 1931, only eighteen months after it was commissioned. This left William Lamb, the chief designer, little time for innovation. The tower was given a conventional central core, and the distance between the exterior windows and the corridor alongside the core was 8.5 metres (29 feet), the maximum depth natural light was then thought to penetrate satisfactorily. New York's zoning laws specified that tall buildings should taper as they rose to avoid cutting off all the light reaching their neighbours, and the Empire State's architects achieved this by incorporating seven set-backs in their design. Each set-back occurred on a floor where one of the low-rise banks of elevators ended its journey and the steel core shrank commensurably, so there was no diminution in the amount of office space available for rent on the upper storeys.

It took just eight months to build the Empire State and it was completed on schedule, a tribute to the practised efficiency of the construction crews who erected it. The new giant had eighty-eight floors including basements; a mooring mast for airships, never used because of the swirling updraughts the building produced, added the equivalent of another fourteen storeys. It was strong and it was attractive, designed in the then fashionable art deco style. Most of all though, it was tall – so lofty at 449 metres (1472 feet) that its mast and upper floors were often enveloped in low cloud.

The cloud base was low on the morning of 28 July 1945 when a B-25 twin-engined bomber piloted by Lieutenant-Colonel W. F. Smith smashed head-on into the middle of the Empire State and tore a hole 6 metres (20 feet) square in the seventy-ninth floor. Both wings sheered off, sending one engine down a lift shaft and the other hurtling through the body of the skyscraper, through the far wall and down on to an adjoining building. Almost immediately, the plane's aviation fuel caught fire and the flames spread, killing Smith, his crew and ten office workers who had their desks on the seventy-ninth floor. One elevator crashed to the sub-basement with the bomber's engine on top of it; it was unoccupied. Another, with two women on board, had its cables severed by flying metal and slipped back down its shaft. The automatic safety devices cut in and the women survived although they were injured. The building itself trembled from the impact of the 10 ton plane – but it stood firm.

Investigations showed that the B-25 had hit the skyscraper right between two of the steel columns that supported the weight of the nine upper floors. One was torn out and the other bent back almost half a metre. However, even if one of the main columns had been destroyed by the crash, the Empire State would have survived almost unscathed. Weight would have been redistributed to the other columns around the edge of the floor and the building would have been dented but left intact. Spectacular as the impact had seemed to those working nearby, the skyscraper had been designed to resist wind forces 200 times greater than the force of the collision. It would take more than a plane crash to damage the world's tallest building.

■ **THE 16 BILLION DOLLAR MAN** Half a century on and half a world away, the team of British architects and Japanese engineers collaborating on the Millennium Tower are designing a building they hope will be a worthy successor to New York's art deco giant. The Empire State holds a particular significance for Keizo Shimizu, the Japanese engineer charged with realizing the project. The New York skyscraper is not only the tallest building he has ever climbed, but also the one he remembers being taught about at school. 'Ever since then,' he said, 'I have dreamed of building the tallest tower in the world. The Empire State Building smashed the record for tall buildings and our dream is to do the same.'

Those school lessons helped to change Shimizu's life. He abandoned his early ambition, to be a harpooner on a whaling ship, and decided that being an engineer

would be just as exciting. It was a wise decision; now in his mid-fifties, he has worked his way up to the position of general manager in the design department of the Obayashi Corporation, one of the five giant companies that dominate the Japanese construction industry and act as developer, architect, consulting engineer and building contractor on hundreds of building projects. In a company that respects conformity, he stands out for his individuality. Short,

Keizo Shimizu, the man in charge of the Obayashi Corporation's design department, wanted to be a harpooner on a whaling ship – but settled for engineering what could become the world's tallest skyscraper.

Left: Plans for the Millennium Tower include cinemas, shops and health centres as well as accommodation.

Above: Obayashi commissioned the British architect Norman Foster to design the Millennium Tower.

He is shown (left) with colleagues David Nelson (in the centre) and Thomas Sheel (on the right).

long-haired and a graduate of both the University of Tokyo and Britain's University of Southampton, he is probably the only man in the whole Obayashi Corporation who wears leather cowboy boots to work. But such eccentricities are ignored, even encouraged, because Shimizu is very good at his job.

The Millennium Tower has been part of his life for seven years, ever since Obayashi commissioned the British architect Norman Foster to design a limit-busting skyscraper far taller than any building in Chicago or New York. With construction costs estimated at no less than $16 billion (£10 billion), no client had dared to commission such a structure. Nevertheless, the Japanese corporation calculated that giant towers would soon be in demand throughout the Far East – they are environmentally and economically viable and generate enormous prestige. If a city or even a limited company did start to look around for a status symbol, Obayashi wanted to be able to offer something truly impressive.

Foster and his associates fulfilled their brief in spectacular style. The Millennium Tower will provide its 50 000 residents and workers with all the necessary comforts and amenities – shops, restaurants, fitness centres and even a hotel – and will require some 20 000 telephone lines and 75 000 kilowatts of electric power. It will be little short of a city in the sky.

The first consideration was to design a structure twice as tall as any other building that would nevertheless stand firm in the face of almost any wind or earthquake that could hit it. At such great heights a conventional square tube tower like the World Trade Centre or the Sears Tower has significant drawbacks. Although the wind pressure at the top of the Millennium Tower will be too weak actually to topple the building it will be strong enough to make an aerodynamically unsound structure sway so noticeably that its occupants would suffer airsickness. Square and rectangular buildings are particularly likely to experience such problems because wind that hits a solid wall head-on breaks up to produce a series of strong eddies and miniature tornadoes, a process known as 'vortex shedding'. The first alternative that Foster and Obayashi considered was a lens-shaped tower, but studies showed that while this would be able to deal comfortably with winds hitting it edge-on, it would be nearly as inefficient as a square tube if the gusts struck it head-on.

The best idea seemed to be a building with a circular cross-section which would produce weaker eddies. Shimizu and Foster's first thought was a cylinder, but they were worried by the problem of earthquakes. Their instincts told them to concentrate the weight of the structure near the ground to add stability. Combining this concept with a cylinder produced a cone with a gross area of more than one million square metres. The engineering justification was there – and so was the added bonus of a building that will be architecturally stunning.

Wind-tunnel tests of its aerodynamic stability showed that the earthquake-derived cone structure was a double winner. Even though a circular cross-section is best for minimizing vortex shedding, there will always be a particular wind speed at which a certain diameter of building will resonate. Because the cone's diameter varies all the way up, only a part of the building will resonate at any given wind speed so the tower will be super-stable. Even so, the 860 metre cone will not be completely immune to wind sway, and Shimizu plans to incorporate two systems in the tower to damp down vibrations. The first will consist of twenty-four large tanks of water, joined in pairs 120 and 150 storeys up. Low levels of vibration will be damped down simply by the principle of inertia, while fiercer gusts can be controlled by pumping water from one tank to the other to counteract any tendency to sway.

As an additional precaution, Obayashi plans to install an invention of its own – AVICS, the Active VIbration Control System – on the 181st floor, close to the top of the tower. AVICS is essentially a more sophisticated version of the water tank damping system, a computer-controlled machine that uses sensors to pick up the tower's motion and instruct a servo motor to shift a horizontal slab of metal mounted on ball screws rapidly from side to side; as the building moves in one direction, the weight is shifted in the other. A slab weighing about 10 tons will damp the motion of a smaller building. The Millennium Tower will have three AVICS installations – enough, Shimizu calculates, to control to-and-fro, lateral and circular sways.

Great strength will nevertheless be vital to the safety of the building. Like other giant skyscrapers built in the last few decades, the Millennium Tower will have a strong external structure as well as a stiff, unyielding core. Twelve criss-cross steel supports will spiral up the outside of the cone, forming an open lattice that will help to damp down winds. For the first 130 floors or so these will be strengthened by ten vertical columns. This conical outer skeleton will protect a cylindrical core that will contain all the tower's office and residential accommodation. The two structures will be joined by gigantic girders, each one floor high, every 30 storeys.

These so-called 'transfer' girders will have two functions. One is to maximize the extent to which the load that bears down on the cylindrical core can be shifted to the strong conical lattice; this conforms to Japanese earthquake regulations which specify that tall buildings should possess strength without undue rigidity. The other is to allow the creation of girder-free 'sky centres', similar to the World Trade Centre's sky lobbies, at regular intervals throughout the Millennium Tower.

The sky centres will divide the skyscraper into five, more manageable, thirty-floor segments and provide each of them with its own leisure facilities, restaurants, shops and public areas. In addition, each one will contain a secure fire-resistant refuge zone large enough to protect the workers and residents of all thirty floors. Emergency stairs and lift shafts will be pressurized to prevent the spread of smoke – an enemy far more deadly than fire in any enclosed space. If any blaze spreads out of the control of the tower's five independent drencher and sprinkler systems, people within the building will be instructed to make their way to the nearest refuge zone, each of which will be protected by double fire walls and smoke prevention enclosures. The zones are rated safe against the fiercest blaze for up to four hours – long enough, Shimizu believes, for his sprinklers to damp down or extinguish the fire or for people to be evacuated in shuttle evacuation lifts.

The Millennium Tower's lift systems have also been designed with the sky centres in mind. Shimizu and his elevator specialists have futuristic plans that should minimize the number of shafts required within the building without compromising safety. Instead of installing conventionally powered lifts, they intend to introduce magnetic linear motor elevators. These will not depend on cables and winches for their power. Instead, enormously powerful electromagnets will push them up and down the lift shafts so quickly that it should take only three minutes to reach the very top of the tower. To maximize carrying capacity, each passenger car will be a double-decker, able to hold 160 people and serve two floors simultaneously. Shimizu will follow the example of the World Trade Centre and use linear motor lifts as express elevators, switching passengers to banks of conventional local ones at each sky centre. However, he intends to go one step further. Sophisticated computers will enable the Millennium Tower to operate several lifts in the same shaft without the risk of collision; and a 'fuzzy logic' management program will direct empty elevators where they are needed, minimizing the time they take to reach waiting passengers.

Right: The brilliant Welsh-American architect Frank Lloyd Wright argued for years against the erection of skyscrapers in city centres – and then startled his supporters with this visionary project for a mile-high monster to be built in Chicago.

Far right: A model of the Millennium Tower – a building that will be a self-contained city in the sky.

Elevator systems are not the only area in which limit-shattering technology is fast revolutionizing the construction of the tallest skyscrapers. Towers such as the Empire State Building were erected by swarms of skilled and semi-skilled workers, but Shimizu believes that much of the Millennium Tower can be built by new generations of mobile robotic factories. Such machines – called Super Construction Factories (SCF) by Obayashi – have already been employed successfully in the construction of smaller buildings and offer significant advantages over traditional manual methods. The SCF is covered and self-contained and can therefore work in any weather and generate minimal levels of noise pollution. It can assemble the basic metal frame for a new building and then place all the necessary beams and floor sections with the help of huge suction pads before moving on. The robot is also mobile and climbs the columns it has just fixed in place to begin work on the next storey.

Although it may seem complicated, climbing is a relatively simply operation. The SCF's support legs are aligned precisely at the spots where columns are required, then one is retracted to the roof of the factory while fully automated cranes and grabs position the new girder. Once this is securely in place, the retracted leg descends again and positions itself over the column. A metal sleeve at the bottom of the leg fits over the girder and ensures that the SCF is held securely in place so that the process can be repeated elsewhere.

Materials needed for construction are delivered to the base of the SCF by forklift truck and crane. The factory's computer brain is pre-programmed with details of the components that are required and where and how they should be fixed. Each item has a bar-code which is scanned as it is lifted into the SCF and placed in a temporary store; when the computer is satisfied that all the materials needed for the construction of the relevant stage have arrived building can commence. As well as grabs, cranes and suction pads, each SCF contains pairs of automated welding machines that are used to fix metal to metal. During the preliminary construction work humans need do little more than fix the occasional bolt and monitor the computer. However, skilled workers are still required to deal with wiring, plumbing and other tasks requiring real dexterity.

Even with the help of every futuristic aid, it could take ten years to build the Millennium Tower – four years of civil works followed by six years of construction. With no client yet firmly committed to the project, this schedule presents a potential problem for Keizo Shimizu, who could reach the end of his working life before his dream can finally be realized. 'It's what I've been living for. If I could at least see the ground-breaking ceremony, though, that would be the high point of my life,' he said. 'And I do believe I will see it, perhaps within the next five years – at any rate before I retire.'

■ **THE HUMAN LIMIT** Finding the billions of dollars needed to build the Millennium Tower is an enormous – perhaps insurmountable – challenge for Obayashi, but when it comes to super-tall buildings the real limit may be human beings. Living or working in skyscrapers presents problems that go beyond merely physical ones like motion sickness and how people react to the air-conditioning and the paradoxical lack of space in a giant building. Just as there are those who feel uncomfortable travelling over a long bridge or through a deep tunnel simply because these structures exceed the limits to which they are accustomed, buildings the size of the Millennium Tower can affront some people.

It is unarguable that giant skyscrapers have many advantages. They save space and generate less pollution than ground-level accommodation for the equivalent number of people. Yet for many years influential architects – notably Frank Lloyd Wright – argued that they are vainglorious, 'molochs raised for commercial greatness' that should be taxed out of existence. Americans, Wright believed, required space and skyscrapers should be built, if built at all, in the countryside where their construction might preserve a green belt from encroaching housing projects.

And yet . . . there is little more alluring than enormous height. Towards the end of his life, even Wright seems to have concurred. In 1956 he shocked his followers by proposing the construction of a skyscraper bigger even than the Millennium Tower: a mile-high building, four times the size of the Empire State, on the waterfront in Chicago: a sky-city capable of housing 120 000 people.

Some said it was a joke, but work had gone into the project; the drawing alone was nearly 7 metres long. And if Wright had at last fallen for the charms of the super-tall building, Keizo Shimizu could understand why. 'I wouldn't mind occupying the top floor, yes,' the Japanese engineer said thoughtfully. 'Looking down on the world, a very beautiful world under our feet, with the clouds and the rain beneath me.'

CHAPTER FIVE

FAST

Years ago, before the Industrial Revolution, the waters of the North Sea were trawled by small wooden boats that hunted its rich fishing grounds for herring. The fish formed part of the staple diet of the people of Britain, Scandinavia and the Low Countries but they were rarely eaten fresh; by the time they reached inland markets they had been heavily salted and packed into barrels. In those days salting was the only way to preserve the fish on their tedious journey from the fishing grounds back to port, from the ships' decks on to the dockside and from the docks out into the countryside beyond. Fresh sea fish were a luxury that was simply not available at a time when ships were generally slow and when ports were relatively inefficient and the infrastructure that connected them to the rest of the country was inadequate.

Even today, these same limits hinder the efficient distribution of commodities that travel by sea. Modern cargo ships may be large and cavernous, but they are built more for economy than speed, and even when they have been unloaded their goods may sit for days awaiting sorting, transportation or customs clearance. Now, however, a British naval designer and his American partners have developed plans that could change all this and lead to the construction of a revolutionary cargo ship so fast that it will be able to carry goods across the Atlantic – and eventually the Pacific – then unload them and see them on their way in a fraction of the time that it takes today.

The proposed new carrier, dubbed FastShip by its creator, David Giles, will be small in comparison to the container ships that currently ply the waters of the North Atlantic. Modern cargo vessels are massive, and fast by the standards that prevailed until only a few decades ago. It is not unusual for one giant to carry the equivalent of 3000 6 metre containers and steam steadily at 20 or 21 knots; but for all their power and capacity, such ships are unsculpted bludgeons that force their way through the waves by brute force and can easily be slowed by bad weather. FastShip, in comparison, will be half the size but twice as quick, a rapier that promises to restore some verve and romance to the sea.

Although the hull shape and form of Giles' creation, and the propulsion system she will use, have a long history, she will be a radical advance over any of her cargo-carrying predecessors. FastShip will be 75 per cent swifter than any other craft of

Previous page: A passenger ferry speeds across the English Channel.

comparable size; and while a few specialist vessels such as hydrofoils and hovercraft may be faster, none is able to maintain its speed for days on end, nor cross one of the roughest of oceans in almost any weather.

FastShip's speed would not be possible using conventional hulls and ordinary diesel engines and propellers. Instead, six great gas-turbine engines, first cousins to the power plants on jumbo jets, will drive massive pumps that suck water from the sea and expel it at speed through the vessel's stern making Giles' creation by far the most powerful ship afloat. A reinforced steel hull of exceptional strength will enable her to force her way through the worst the stormy North Atlantic can throw at her without sacrificing a speed of more than 40 knots.

Giles calculates such power and speed will enable FastShip to make a return journey across the Atlantic in only a week – more than twice the speed of the best service currently offered by a conventional container ship – and reach port within a few minutes of her scheduled arrival time on ninety-nine crossings out of 100. Such punctuality, unheard of in shipping circles, holds out the tantalizing prospect of completely reliable deliveries of high-value goods to customers who have previously been forced to hoard substantial stocks and accept the probability of delays. FastShip therefore has the potential, Giles insists, to save them the cost of holding millions of pounds worth of inventory to guard against unforeseen contingencies and revolutionize industry as surely as she will transform the international freighting community.

It is no coincidence that the engineer responsible for this remarkable project has a background in aircraft projects and sailing boats rather than conventional naval architecture. Giles began his working career with a short spell as a submariner, and he still possesses the clipped accent of a naval officer and the no-nonsense efficiency of a seaman. A graduate (in arts) of Oxford University his aeronautical education began when he joined the de Havilland aircraft company in 1961 to work on the highly successful DH–125 aircraft project. The new plane was born from the harsh lessons of project engineering the company had been taught by its predecessor, the Comet I – an aircraft that had been an aerodynamic success but a commercial and engineering disaster.

'The problem with the Comet I was that nobody brought it together,' is Giles' analysis of the disaster. 'The de Havilland organization was full of departments with their own priorities and ambitions, and you really need somebody who is, I think, able both to understand the technical issues and arguments, and above all the personalities. You need to be more than just an engineer to do something like that.'

The 125, which at first seemed destined to follow its predecessor into obscurity, became perhaps the most successful product of the all-British commercial aircraft industry. Giles, also caught up in airliner programmes, learnt about commercial realities and customer relations as well as engineering techniques. 'I had to understand what the American market wanted and what we could deliver,' he recalled, 'and how those two could be reconciled.' The result of this experience is a lean collaboration between his company, Thornycroft Giles, which has a few key staff in the United Kingdom (four designers and their computers can now do the jobs of forty old-fashioned draughtsmen), a twelve-man Danish commercial ship design team and a small, Virginia-based American partner, FastShip Atlantic. Funding is likely to come from the United States government and manufacturers who will use the new service, and there are plans to contract much of the work of building the new vessels out to United States shipyards that will work under imported European management.

In short, FastShip will be an international effort and a notable collaboration between engineers and entrepreneurs from the United States, Europe and the United Kingdom. It is a far cry from the days when a generation of merchant ships was last built expressly for speed, when wind was the premier motive power, local shipyards guarded the secrets of their designs, and there was no such thing as a common body of knowledge of naval architecture.

Above: FastShip will make a return trip from Belgium to America within a week.

Right: As a designer of aircraft and yachts Giles has significant advantages over conventional naval architects.

■ **ALL THE TEA IN CHINA** Tea was one of the very few commodities that were carried at speed in the heyday of sail. Most other cargoes were either too bulky or insufficiently valuable to be worth the risks involved in skittering through the typhoons and treacherous shoals of the China Sea with all sails set in order to dock in the Port of London a few hours or days ahead of the pack. But in the middle years of the nineteenth century demand for fresh tea was such that the first vessel to return from Foochow or Shanghai could command a premium of at least 10 per

鎌　倉

KAMAKURA
PANAMA

Cargo on the deck of a container ship – a vessel whose massive capacity is not matched by a sparkling performance at sea.

cent for her wares; and a clipper ship which cost perhaps £12 000 or £15 000 to build might bring home a cargo worth almost £3000 on her first voyage.

The clipper is probably the least 'scientific' of all the inventions described in this book. The men who built them and other merchant ships were artists rather than engineers. Some designers may have known of the engineer John Scott Russell and his wave-line theory, the first modern mathematical statement of the relationship between hull design and speed, but no two ships built in any yard were truly alike, and often only time could tell which would prove good sailors and which would disappoint. Although models of each new vessel were built, they were used for guidance when laying out a vessel's lines rather than in tests. When William Hall – the Aberdonian master shipbuilder who designed the prototype clipper *Scottish Maid* in 1839 – proposed to test his new idea for a sharper bow by sailing a model in a tank, his decision raised eyebrows in Aberdeen's other yards.

Hall was one of the most important figures in the development of fast sailing ships and his 'Aberdeen bow', which added speed without limiting cargo capacity, soon inspired imitations. The earliest true clipper hulls, however, appear to have evolved independently in both the United States and Scotland. An American merchantman, the *Rainbow* of 1845, is often described as the first of the clipper breed, and when her immediate successor, the *Oriental*, made her appearance at Hong Kong in 1850 she created a sensation in local shipping circles. The cause of the furore was the news that she had made the passage out from New York in the record time of eighty-one days. She was immediately offered a substantial premium – 25 per cent – on the prevailing freight rates to accept a charter for London. Loaded with almost 1650 tons of tea, the *Oriental* left Whampoa, the tea port north of Hong Kong, on 27 August 1850 and sailed south against the monsoons. She reached the West India Dock in London on 4 December, only ninety-nine days after leaving China. By way of comparison, the British opium clipper *Astarte* sailed from Whampoa only a day later than her rival but took a month longer to reach her destination. It took British shipbuilders several years to match the *Oriental*.

Further innovations were introduced into clipper designs. The increasing demand for tea, a relatively light but highly valuable cargo, made it possible to hollow out the ships' lines. This limited the capacity of the holds but produced a more pronounced 'rise of floor' – the slope at which the hull angles outwards from the central keel to the ship's sides – which reduced water resistance and helped the ship to sail faster when heeled over under sail.

The long, lean lines of a clipper ship were far more efficient than those of an East Indiaman, built for cargo capacity and strength. They also permitted considerable savings in weight. Shipbuilders were always concerned to place the masts as far apart as possible to ensure that the sails of one did not blanket those of another and so reduce speed. On a squat East Indiaman the foremast was placed far forward and often raked ahead at an angle as well to maximize its distance from the mainmast. The heavy weight of this mast and its spars and equipment added to the stresses placed on the bow when it was intermittently suspended over the trough of a wave, and could eventually force the whole stem – the forepart – of the ship downwards, producing a condition known as 'hogging' which significantly reduced efficiency. To compensate, the bow itself was often massively reinforced. The designer of a long clipper ship could place her foremast well back from the bow, which largely eradicated the problem of hogging and allowed the introduction of much lighter and more efficient bows.

The new bow swept rakishly forward at an angle of up to 50 degrees and was one of the clipper's most distinctive features. Most significantly, however, it helped the ship to maintain her speed in heavy weather. Its finer lines meant that she encountered far less resistance than other ships to her passage through the water; instead of progressing in a series of checks and shocks as she encountered wave after wave until her stern was buried and her crew forced to reduce sail for fear of being swamped, a clipper could cut through the swells. It took heavier weather to slow her and on a long voyage she would therefore maintain a much higher average speed. The only problem with the British clipper bow was that it often had too little sheer – the upward curve towards the bowsprit – and little distance between the deck and water-line so that when the ship did nose dive the bowmen could be washed overboard and drowned.

Blowing and cracking from the masts were the huge white sails that pushed a clipper forward. The flourishing of the China trade crowned centuries of trial and error with masts and sails, and the power that a clipper could draw from a following wind with all sails set was far greater than anything that could be supplied by contemporary steam engines. A vessel might touch 16 knots in the best conditions, and average 11 or 12 knots in reasonable weather, at a time when the steam fleet made 8 or 9 knots and would need to take on coal four or five times on a passage between Britain and China.

A typical clipper ship of the late 1860s had three masts, each of which was fitted (looking from the bottom up) with a lower course sail, double topsails, single or double topgallants, a royal and a skysail. A crack ship could easily set thirty or more sails in the most favourable conditions. Their quality was vital to the performance of the ship; the best were made of heavy cotton duck or flax canvas.

As well as concentrating his attentions on a sail plan, a designer would also devote much attention to smoothing the underwater part of the hull at the after end. This practice lessened friction and added speed – but it had its dangers. Too clean a run could mean that the stern did not have sufficient overhang above the water-line when chased by waves, and the consequent lack of buoyancy often led to a ship being pooped – that is, swamped by a following wave.

Clippers, like more conservatively built ships, were generally loaded so that they were heavier at the stern, as the extra weight was thought to help their sailing qualities. Nevertheless, once a cargo had been stowed away, the crew would still have to work hard to redistribute it so as to ensure the optimum speed.

These then were the ships that, in the days of the China tea trade, competed to be the first to deliver their precious cargoes to England.

■ **THE GREAT RACE OF 1866** Each year, in the 1860s and 1870s, the crack vessels of the clipper fleet would race each other to be first home to London. Such contests were never official, but they were heavily fought nonetheless and much rested on their outcome, both for the merchants whose profits depended on the performance of their ships and for the captains who often wagered heavily on who would have the honour of leading the fleet home. Of all the Tea Races, that of 1866 was the greatest and most exciting. There were perhaps a dozen clippers that aspired to win it, but the leading contender was *Ariel*, the fleetest vessel of her time. Using her 30 300 square feet of canvas, she was capable of reaching speeds of 16 knots, far faster than those of contemporary steamers.

Yet the start of the race was not auspicious for the *Ariel* or her master, John Keay. Although Keay had triumphed over his fellow-captains in securing the first cargo to come on the market at the great Chinese port of Foochow, and been the first master to sail for London that year, he had been unlucky with his tugs. The paddle steamer *Island Queen*, hired to take *Ariel* in tow, lacked the power to carry her across the bar of the Min River against a falling tide, and Keay, his ship and crew were forced to lie at anchor and watch as other clippers completed their hurried loading and started in pursuit.

That evening their rival, *Fiery Cross*, came down the river towed by a more powerful tug, edged her way over the bar and set a course east across the China Sea. Keay was still negotiating the bar with the help of the *Island Queen* next morning when two other clippers, *Serica* and *Taeping*, appeared alongside him.

Keay must have realized that he would have to call on all of *Ariel*'s fine qualities to win that season's Tea Race and maximize the value of his cargo for her owners. *Fiery Cross*, built six years earlier, had proved herself by far the fastest and most successful clipper of the early 1860s, while his craft was comparatively untried. Although slightly smaller than *Ariel*, the ship now receding into the dusk of the China Sea boasted elegant hollow lines that made her a good sailer into the wind, and her master, Dick Robinson, had fitted her with all kinds of gear to improve the efficiency of her sails. Moreover, Robinson was a highly experienced racer who had brought *Fiery Cross* home to London first in the Tea Races of 1861, 1862, 1863 and 1865 and had been beaten in 1864 only by the brand-new *Serica*. His anxiety at the early departure of the *Ariel* had been so great that he had weighed anchor the moment his cargo was complete, without his papers and without signing the cargo manifest. This gained him twelve hours on the *Taeping* and the *Serica* – and reduced the latter's master, Captain Innes, to an apoplectic fury.

The four ships sailed east to round the northern coast of Formosa, then set a course to the south. Occasionally they came close enough for the crew of one ship to see the men of another setting more sails or trimming their vessel to coax an extra quarter-knot from her, but for most of the time the rival clippers sailed independently. *Fiery Cross* made good use of the fourteen-hour lead she had gained over *Ariel* at the bar of the Min River and reached Anjer, at the exit to the China Sea, only twenty days out from Foochow. *Taeping* and *Ariel* had fallen two days behind and *Serica* passed the town a day after them. But favourable weather in the Indian Ocean and around the Cape of Good Hope evened matters out somewhat

and all four ships made fine time. *Ariel* logged a single day's run of 530 miles and *Fiery Cross* one of 528 miles. By the time the island of St Helena came over the horizon, Captain MacKinnon's *Taeping* held a slender lead of twenty-four hours over *Fiery Cross*, with *Ariel* and *Serica* one day further behind.

Three of the four rival clippers were composite ships built of wood over an iron frame, but *Serica* was lighter. She was wood only and had finer lines than *Taeping*, her half-sister. Her captain was a notoriously hard taskmaster as well as being a man of volcanic temper, and in the lighter winds that were encountered around the Equator he caught up with *Taeping*. *Ariel* was also picking up speed and all four vessels passed Flores, in the Azores, together on 29 August.

The wind remained fair, blowing from the south-east, as the racers headed for the English Channel. As the four ships gradually strung out into a line luck or determination slightly favoured *Ariel* and *Taeping* over *Fiery Cross* and *Serica*. Still neck and neck after ninety-seven days at sea, the two leaders ran up the channel in sight of each other, both logging 14 knots for most of the day as they made for Deal

The Tea Race of 1866 was won by *Taeping* but *Ariel*, the fastest clipper of her day, was only 25 minutes behind.

and the Tea Race's unofficial finishing post. At eight on the morning of 6 September watchers on shore spotted *Ariel* signalling her number and less than ten minutes later *Taeping* hove into view to claim second place. *Serica* was less than two hours behind her, with *Fiery Cross* an unlucky and (to Robinson) humiliating thirty-six hours further back. Even then, the racers were reluctant to abandon the competition and, with Keay again unlucky in his choice of tug, *Taeping* was able to nip into the London docks twenty-five minutes ahead of *Ariel*. *Serica* reached port that same evening, but failed to share in the 10 shillings per ton premium awarded to the first tea of the season, which was split between *Ariel* and *Taeping*.

The Tea Race of 1866 caused an enormous stir in Britain's sporting and nautical circles. *Ariel* and *Taeping* had left Foochow together and arrived home on the other side of the globe still together, *Ariel*'s time being a minuscule seven-thousandths of one per cent faster than her rival – yet that extra speed had earned her owner hundreds of pounds.

The Tea Race was never so close again in all its thirty-year history.

■ **SEA WITCH** As the tea trade continued to flourish into the late 1860s, clipper design became both more refined and more extreme, culminating in the construction of two vessels whose perfect lines and great rivalry illuminated the final flickerings of the age of sail. Their names were *Thermopylae* and *Cutty Sark*, and although they were in many respects obsolete practically as soon as they were launched, they remain two of the finest examples of large sailing ships designed for speed.

Thermopylae, the elder of the two, was built in Aberdeen and launched in 1868. Her underwater lines were especially fine and smooth and she carried plenty of sail. Her canvas was deeper than that of her predecessors – her mainsail alone was more than 40 feet from top to bottom – and this added substantially to her power. She excelled in light winds, particularly going into the wind, and it was said that she could do 7 knots in a breeze so slight that a man could walk around her deck with a lighted candle. In heavier winds she made one day's run of 348 miles at an average speed of $14\frac{1}{2}$ knots.

Cutty Sark also embodied the lessons tea traders had learned in the previous two decades. Built in Dumbarton in Scotland and launched in 1869, her design was said to have been based on that of a French frigate. Her underwater lines were exceptionally smooth and, like Giles' FastShip, her entrance – the forepart of the part of the hull that was under water – was deep and unusually long and straight. *Cutty Sark*'s stern overhung the rudder by several feet, which added a margin of safety when she was running before heavy seas. She could carry an enormous quantity of sail and was perhaps the fastest of all the tea clippers, touching $17\frac{1}{2}$ knots and maintaining a speed of 15 to 16 knots – a knot or two faster than most of her rivals – in ideal conditions. Her full suit of sails is estimated to have generated a remarkable 3000 horsepower, ten times more than the engine of the fastest contemporary racing steamer, and her best day's run of 362 miles was one of the longest recorded. Not surprisingly, for a vessel whose entrance closely resembled that of FastShip, she did not slow in high seas and was at her fastest with the wind up, when the flow of water under her hull helped to provide stability. In conditions like these not a clipper afloat could keep up with her.

Both *Cutty Sark* and *Thermopylae* began their careers loading tea at Wusung, just north of Shanghai, and Foochow. In 1870, when bad weather prevented many fast runs home, *Cutty Sark* made London in 110 days, while her rival was five days faster. The next year, sailing two months apart, *Thermopylae*'s lead was a week. But the Tea Race of 1872 was perhaps the most closely contested and dramatic since 1866. The two clippers left Shanghai on 18 June and raced together down the China Sea. When they passed Anjer thirty-one days later *Thermopylae* had a lead of just $1\frac{1}{2}$ miles. The passage west across the Indian Ocean favoured *Cutty Sark*, however, and by the time she rounded the Cape of Good Hope she had built a lead of 400 miles, enough to give her an excellent chance of winning the race.

Unfortunately for Captain Moodie and his crew, *Cutty Sark*'s thousands of miles of hard sailing were about to catch up with her. As she rounded the South African coast to set a course north for home, her rudder groaned, cracked and gave way. Moodie was forced to heave to and it took the ship's company six days to build and rig a temporary rudder. They continued under reduced sail and, thus handicapped, *Cutty Sark* hobbled north. Her speed was no more than 8 knots and her lead over *Thermopylae* was steadily eroded until, by the time she made St Helena, her rival had passed her and built a lead of five days. However, *Cutty Sark*'s sailing qualities were such that Captain Kemball of *Thermopylae* was unable to add substantially to his advantage even though both ships had to cover thousands of

miles before completing the race. He docked at London on 11 October after 115 days at sea, only a week ahead of Moodie and his clipper.

Cutty Sark was to have her revenge in the mid-1880s when both she and *Thermopylae* switched from the tea trade to running Australian wool between New South Wales and London. She found the heavy weather in the Roaring Forties of the southern hemisphere much to her taste, recorded some remarkably fast times and comfortably beat *Thermopylae* with her liking for lighter winds. A new master, Captain Richard Woodget, had taken over from a succession of indifferent men. He drove a crack crew hard and got the best out of them, so that in 1888 *Cutty Sark*

Cutty Sark, perhaps the most beautiful sailing ship ever built, and certainly one of the most efficient, is seen here with all sails set. Her canvas could generate more than 3000 horsepower – ten times that available to the fastest racing steamer of the day.

made a run of only seventy-one days from Newcastle, the chief Australian wool port, to Cape Dungeness on England's south coast.

Cutty Sark and *Thermopylae* were carrying Australian wool because the route out to China had been dominated since the early 1870s by a new generation of fast steamers. Although their best speeds were less than those of a crack clipper, they were more reliable, steaming on for hour after hour in conditions in which any sailing ship would be becalmed. When the clippers arrived at Foochow and Shanghai in the spring of 1870, they found many racing steamers that had come out via Suez in half the usual time already there. Steamers such as the *Hiparchus* and *Achilles* made the voyage back to London in only sixty days, coaling stops included, and could command much higher fees for shipping their cargoes. Their sailing rivals had to cut their fees commensurably and were eventually forced away to ports that steam had not yet reached. Towards the end of the 1870s Yokohoma in Japan and Manila in the Philippines were more common destinations than the familiar waters of Shanghai and Foochow. A decade later, even these ports were thronged with iron freighters belching smoke and shuddering from the vibrations of their reciprocating engines. The greatest flourish of the sailing merchantmen was over; for all their grace and beauty, they had been driven out of business by faster ships.

■ **PADDLES AND PROPELLERS** Steam propulsion had first made its appearance late in the eighteenth century and became increasingly prevalent after 1815. For many years there were considerable teething problems. Safe engines worked at low pressure and delivered low performance, while the more powerful, high-pressure engines required to improve performance significantly were dangerous and prone to explosions. Fuel was expensive, particularly to a generation accustomed to the free power provided by the wind, and its consumption was initially high enough to limit the range of steam-powered ships to a few hundred miles – well short of what would be needed for an ocean crossing. Fur-

Isambard Kingdom Brunel outshone even his father Marc in the public eye. He built railways, designed the Clifton Suspension Bridge and was the architect of three of the most revolutionary steamers of the nineteenth century.

thermore, the paddle-wheel, the first method of waterborne steam propulsion to be perfected, was initially inefficient. Only a few of its blades were in contact with the water at any one time, the bulky paddle-boxes seriously affected the streamlining of the ship's hull – and the engines and paddles took up space that could be allocated to freight on a merchantman, or to armament on a warship.

Nevertheless, the paddle-wheel eventually achieved a considerable degree of sophistication. In 1832 a Nova Scotian steamer, *Royal William*, became the first vessel to cross the Atlantic with her engines working all the way – although with her sails also set – and six years later an altogether more advanced vessel, *Great Western*, inaugurated the first regular powered service between Britain and the United States.

The wonderful new paddle-wheeler was the creation of that remarkable polymath Isambard Kingdom Brunel, the only son of Sir Marc Brunel and one of the principal engineers of the great railway boom of the 1830s and 1840s. Like Giles' FastShip, the *Great Western* was intended from the beginning to revolutionize transatlantic shipping by setting new standards for speed and reliability. And like FastShip she offered improved links to the national infrastructure – she was to be an extension of Brunel's Great Western railway, which ran from Paddington in London to the port of Bristol.

Isambard Brunel was the first man to realize that an unassisted steam passage of the Atlantic was practicable. His contemporaries believed that no ship could carry enough fuel to make the crossing; and that building bigger ones would be no answer because a larger vessel would need proportionately more power to drive it, and thus more fuel. Brunel's genius was to recognize that while the power required to drive a hull through the water is proportional to area and increases as the square of its dimensions, its carrying capacity, which is related to volume, increases as the cube. A large ship can therefore stow a significantly larger proportion of fuel. *Great Western*, launched in Bristol in 1837, was the product of this simple maxim: a steamer of unprecedented size designed expressly for the Atlantic service. She was 236 feet long and displaced 1200 tons – tiny by modern standards – and her paddle-wheels were driven by a pair of Maudslay engines which delivered 750 horsepower and were nearly twice as powerful as anything else afloat.

As well as being a remarkable engineering achievement in her own right,

Brunel's ship was the pride of Bristol and the city's deliberate assault on the Atlantic passenger trade which was at that time dominated by London and Liverpool. And Liverpool and London were determined to strike back. When they heard that *Great Western* was being fitted out in London for her maiden voyage, shippers from the these ports chartered their own steamers in an attempt to steal the glory of a successful crossing. Lack of time drove them to desperate lengths. The Londoners' charter, *Sirius*, was a steam-packet that had never been designed for the Atlantic. Nevertheless, this little 700 ton paddler managed to board forty passengers and slip away from the capital on 28 March 1838. She was three days ahead of the *Great Western* and the contender from Liverpool was nowhere in sight.

Brunel and his crew hurried down the Thames after *Sirius* and headed for Bristol where they were to embark their own passengers for the crossing. They were only a few hours out when near disaster struck. Felt boiler lagging was ignited by heat from the furnaces and caused a dangerous outbreak of fire which forced Captain Claxton to ground his ship on Canvey Island in the Thames estuary until the flames were extinguished. Twelve precious hours were lost. When *Great Western* finally reached Bristol it was to discover that news of the fire had spread and only seven brave passengers were prepared to chance their lives and board the untried ship for her Atlantic crossing.

Brunel's ship therefore headed west five days behind her rival – and, like her, steamed into the teeth of the spring equinoctial gales. The weather was so bad that the passengers and crew on board *Sirius* feared their ship would be overwhelmed and implored her captain to turn about. This he refused to do, and the steam-packet successfully weathered the storm. *Sirius* steamed into New York after nineteen days at sea with her bunkers filled with little but dust. Legend has it that the passage was only completed by feeding the ship's wooden fittings into the furnaces. This is an exaggeration but, with only 15 tons of coal in reserve, *Sirius* proved – even in her moment of triumph – that a reliable Atlantic steam service could only be provided by a larger vessel. When *Great*

From Hendon farmer to internationally respected inventor of the screw propeller, Francis Pettit Smith's career led him from experiments on his duck pond to sea-going trials of strength between screw steamers and paddle-wheelers.

Western reached New York less than a day later, her bunkers were still a quarter full and she had made up most of the distance by making the passage at just under 9 knots, 2 knots faster than *Sirius*. This successful performance encouraged sixty-eight passengers to sail with her on the return voyage and the first regular steam service across the Atlantic was inaugurated. *Great Western* was the first vessel to wear the coveted Blue Ribband awarded to the fastest passenger-carrying ship to cross the Atlantic.

However, the great paddler's success was illusory. By the time she made her first crossing, a new form of propulsion had nearly been perfected – one that continues to dominate the sea-lanes today, and may eventually be bettered only by the water jets planned for Giles' FastShip. This was the screw propeller.

The concept of driving vessels with a screw mounted on a drive shaft that projected aft was old by the time Victoria came to the throne in 1837. It had been invented independently more than a dozen times between 1804 and 1833; even Marc Brunel had experimented with the idea. But want of engineering expertise, funds or influence doomed each project to failure and systematic experiments were made and funds allocated to promoting the propeller only when Francis Pettit Smith, a farmer from Hendon north of London, began to take an interest.

Smith began by building a 24 inch model which he sailed on a duck pond on his farm. By September 1837 he had progressed to a small launch, 33 feet long. Unlike modern propellers, which comprise a number of blades mounted on a central boss, Smith's prototype consisted of a long axis around which twisted two rotations of a single blade. By chance, half the blade snapped off during trials and the propeller's performance improved markedly. This provided the first real clues to efficient screw design and allowed the launch to steam from Gravesend at the mouth of the Thames to Margate on the Kent coast in only seven hours, returning in weather so poor that paddle-steamers could not venture out.

Smith's genius lay not so much in his design for a propeller – others were rather more efficient – but in his instinct for positioning it correctly. A rival invention by a Swede, John Ericsson, had been rejected by the Admiralty on the grounds that its position behind the rudder would make it very difficult to steer the ship. Smith placed his just forward of the rudder, an inspired decision which not only allowed the propeller to operate in water which had been slowed down and calmed by the friction of its passage along the hull, but actually improved the steering. This was because the rotation of the propeller generated a mass of water which flowed directly on to the rudder and made the latter respond to the helm more quickly.

Smith's next step, in 1839, was to build *Archimedes*, a seagoing vessel that would embody his latest ideas and prove the superiority of the screw by racing against four other steamers – including the Dover steam-packet *Widgeon*, the fastest paddle-steamer in the English Channel. The Royal Navy also ordered trials of the propeller to obtain data and to win public approval for the new invention. Two new ships, the screw steamer *Rattler* and the paddler *Alecto*, were built with identical hulls and engines of the same power. They were then matched against each other in a series of races in varying weather conditions and over a number of distances. *Rattler* proved herself superior in each instance. The final trial was a spectacular tug-of-war which became one of the most celebrated naval incidents of the nineteenth century. The ships were lashed together stern to stern; then, while *Rattler* lay idle, *Alecto* started her engine and, her paddle-wheels thrashing at the sea, slowly got under way until she was making 2 knots with *Rattler* swaying along behind her. Then the screw vessel joined the contest. Her propeller spun at its maximum speed and *Alecto*'s forward motion was gradually slowed, then halted. Eventually, for all the commotion of her straining paddles, she was towed helplessly astern by the propeller-driven ship.

Smith's *Archimedes*, meanwhile, was responsible for the development of the first great screw steamer. After a successful showing against *Widgeon* she was sent on a promotional tour that took her right around the British Isles. Along the way she called at Bristol where Brunel and his steamship company were contemplating a successor for *Great Western*. Their new vessel would be twice the size of any ship afloat – a gigantic iron paddler of no less than 3400 tons. The arrival of *Archimedes* brought them up short. Her trials at Bristol were a revelation to Brunel who chartered her for six months and made a highly detailed examination of the principles of screw propulsion. Plans for paddle-wheels were dropped. The big steamer was given a propeller and a name: *Great Britain*. She was the first modern ship.

Around Bristol the new vessel was known as 'Mammoth'. She was 325 feet long and 50 feet broad, only just small enough to fit the locks at the port's docks; indeed she jammed in them shortly after launching. But in addition to her sheer

size, *Great Britain* was given what amounted to clipper lines: a sharply pointed bow that was concave at the water-line, a smooth run aft along her bottom and a fine stern – features that made her potentially very fast. There were no fewer than six masts and 16 145 square feet of sail to provide auxiliary propulsion, while a single six-bladed screw no less than $15\frac{1}{2}$ feet in diameter turned at up to fifty-three revolutions per minute. This propeller, designed after Brunel had conducted extensive experiments on board *Archimedes*, was driven by a 2000 horsepower engine and could propel the iron ship at up to 12 knots under steam alone. The engine, too, was novel. Brunel had been heavily critical of the noisy and inefficient gearing system employed in *Archimedes'* engine, and he replaced this with a gigantic chain drive that weighed 7 tons. The hull that contained this advanced piece of engineering was unprecedentedly strong thanks to Brunel's insistence on substantial longitudinal strength, and its general arrangement and provision of five watertight bulkheads look surprisingly modern even today. There was plenty of room for 360 passengers and 21 900 cubic feet of cargo.

Like *Great Western*, *Great Britain* was an enormously ambitious leap forward in design; indeed it has been said that only Brunel would have dared to incorporate

In 1845 the Royal Navy sponsored trials between *Alecto*, fitted with paddle-wheels and *Rattler*, with a propeller. In the final trial, the two ships were secured stern to stern and sailed away at full steam. *Rattler's* screw won the day; she towed her sister backwards at 2 knots and proved the superiority of propeller over paddle-wheel.

quite so many revolutionary ideas in a single ship. It is perhaps not surprising that potential passengers were as worried by her as they had been by her predecessor – on her maiden voyage in August 1845 she was only an eighth full. Nevertheless, the passage to New York was completed without incident, in just under fourteen days and at an average speed of 9.4 knots. It is interesting that *Great Britain*'s best day's run on this occasion was only 287 miles, substantially less than a tea clipper could make across the Indian Ocean.

Great Britain was not destined to enjoy a happy life. Throughout her career she proved to be under-powered and suffered a succession of problems with her propellers. On her second transatlantic journey her massive but weakly constructed screw disintegrated blade by blade during the return voyage and she was compelled to finish under sail. The propeller was replaced with a stronger and more efficient four-bladed screw and she returned to service, but on her next passage her captain made an elementary navigational error and ran her firmly aground on the Irish coast. She remained there, stuck fast, for almost a year; only the exceptional strength of her construction saved her from destruction. Even so, the disaster bankrupted Brunel's Great Western Steamship Company. The great ship was sold and, after ferrying troops to the Crimea, spent the rest of her career carrying emigrants out to Australia. Ironically, on these voyages her sails were more valuable to her than her screw. She ended her working days stranded in the Falkland Islands in the South Atlantic where only Brunel's enormously strong hull kept her intact long enough for her final salvage in 1970 – and her eventual return to Bristol where, now refurbished, she can once again be visited.

■ **BY JET ACROSS THE ATLANTIC** The initial success of *Great Britain* sealed the reputation of the screw as the most effective method of propelling an engined vessel. But it gradually became plain that the propeller itself had significant drawbacks when it came to driving the fastest of ships. Even the swiftest screw-driven craft are pressed to reach 40 knots or more, and those that do tend to be sleek warships rather than bulky cargo carriers. To shift significant quantities of freight at very high speed will require a new form of propulsion, one as revolutionary as the propeller was in its day – and David Giles

This computer simulation of David Giles' FastShip gives some idea of her huge size and impressive build.

believes that he has found this in the water jets that he will use for his FastShip.

'Propellers are not efficient above 35 knots because they have to be scaled up to an unmanageable size,' he explained. 'The propellers on the *QEII* deliver about 40 000 horsepower but FastShip needs about 320 000 in total. To obtain that sort of power you would need two screws perhaps 8 to 10 metres in diameter, and at that size they would be very vulnerable to damage; you would also experience terrific problems of torque and pitch. Aircraft have the same limits – even turboprops are only efficient up to about 350 knots and after that jet engines take over. Water jets will be 25 per cent more efficient than propellers at 40 knots.'

The idea of using water jets at sea was first proposed at the beginning of the nineteenth century, and jet-powered ferries capable of FastShip's speed are already in service today. What is new is the sheer size of the engines available and their adaptation to a route – across the stormy waters of the North Atlantic – that is far more challenging than any so far tackled by a jet ship.

The *Great Britain* could carry 360 passengers and had space for nearly 22 000 square feet of cargo. She made her first passage to New York in under fourteen days at an average speed of just over 9 knots.

FastShip will be powered by water jets driven by six gas-turbine engines of the latest type – far more up to date than the 1950s and 1960s designs still favoured by the United States Navy and the Royal Navy, and together worth about $82 million, 50 per cent of the estimated value of each ship. Two of the six gas turbines will be coupled to drive the main water jet booster, generating around 41 megawatts of power – and four will be used for manouvring. Working together, FastShip's engines will produce enough energy to power a medium-sized town – or send Giles' creation across the Atlantic at average speeds of about 40 knots.

Although they are far from efficient at speeds below 22 knots, water jets powered by turbines are much smaller and lighter than diesel engines and therefore leave more room for cargo. In addition, the water jet outlets can be angled so that their thrust can be directed and even reversed, making FastShip highly manoeuvrable. The water jets will scoop water from the surrounding sea and use the gas turbines' power to drive impellers that expel the water through huge vents at the stern. Each outlet pipe will be 4 metres in diameter – tall enough to drive a bus through. This is so much larger than the biggest so far built, which has a diameter of only 1.2 metres, that Giles will need to ensure that careful experiments are conducted to satisfy himself they can be made strong enough to withstand the stress of constant use.

Giles' enthusiasm for his water jet propulsion system is infectious but many naval architects have questioned whether FastShip's engines will prove to be simply too powerful. The ship's stern will have to be very strongly fixed to the rest of the hull to endure the huge stresses generated by the jets. And sceptics have argued that FastShip will not be capable of travelling at constant high speeds through heavy seas without breaking up.

Moving a large ship through stormy weather at high speed requires a large quantity of expensive fuel and FastShip is expected to burn up to ten times as much oil as a conventional container ship – up to 4600 tons per crossing. Giles expects to balance these additional running costs by making up to five times as many Atlantic crossings a year as existing vessels. But to do so his ship will have to be extremely tough and designed as efficiently as possible.

FastShip's high-speed hull – one of the most radical innovations in naval architecture since the introduction of clipper lines – is perhaps its most novel feature. It is long – wave-tank tests have shown its optimum length to be around

263 metres, two and a half times the size of *Great Britain* – with a beam of 40 metres. A sharp bow, rounded underside and flat, cut-off stern make FastShip look like nothing so much as a gigantic, ocean-going yacht. But the real secret of the hull's speed lies hidden under water, where it curves upwards from a deep bow to produce a subtly concave stern. As the ship gains speed water rushing along its bottom will be forced along this hollow to create lift. The same effect will help to force water into the jet inlet pipes which will improve their efficiency.

The upward push of water at the stern should offer FastShip a revolutionary advantage over conventional vessels. Naval architects have long struggled to overcome the problem of drag which develops at high speeds as a ship powering through the sea creates bigger and bigger waves while, at the same time, its stern is sucked down into its own wake creating a definable limit to its potential speed.

'What this hull really tends to do is create its own wave with its stern,' Giles explained. 'As an ordinary ship goes faster, the whole stern starts to sink and the drag curve starts to go up almost vertically. What we're doing is just simply stopping that happening so that drag increases as a constant effect of speed. FastShip produces what I call a self-sustaining wave – as the ship goes faster and the tendency to trim or to sink at the stern increases, the size of the wave created at the stern increases and so the whole thing balances out.

'There are other advantages. The pressure under the hull reduces drag and gets the water jets to about 75 per cent efficiency. Then, because of the lift produced at the stern, the whole ship can be made wider in the beam. That in turn gives more room for the water jets and for cargo to be loaded and unloaded. At the same time, the high pressure under the hull dampens the ship's motion in pitch and roll and the sea at the bows simply disintegrates into a spray without producing significant drag. I call the whole effect a Virtuous Circle.'

Like the principle of the water jet, the concave hull form is not new. It appears to have been conceived by Sir John Thornycroft, whose Southampton-based shipyard built some of the fastest torpedo boats, motor boats and destroyers to see service with the Royal Navy, and was introduced in the power boat *Gyrinus*. This small launch, only 11½ metres long, competed in the 1908 Olympic Games – which included power boat races – where she won two gold medals and reached speeds of almost 22 knots. With her round bilge, petrol engine and rails fitted along her sides at the water-line to provide lift and prevent sinking, she was the first vessel to have a semi-planing hull.

In 1989 Giles applied for a patent on 'semi-planing monohulls' of over 2000 tons displacement, initially in the United States and, later, in Europe and elsewhere. The United States and European patents have now been issued, providing FastShip with a degree of design and market protection without which, Giles states, he would probably not have proceeded. It is almost unprecedented for such a radical change in transportation to enjoy the benefit of such protection. This restricts, for a period, the inevitable over-capacity which tends to swamp the market when any good new idea – such as the container – comes along. 'Think what it would have meant to de Havilland if they had been able to patent the jet liner,' Giles said.

Testing the strength of a vessel in a wave tank is an essential element in the design of a ship. In FastShip's case doing this was additional to intensive computer simulations that tested her design in every kind of sea condition.

FastShip's carefully designed hull is the product of intensive computer simulations supplemented by an ongoing programme of tank testing. The computer work was performed at the famous Massachusetts Institute of Technology by Professor Paul Sclavounos, a hydrodynamicist and naval architect, who was partly responsible for the lines of *Young America*, the yacht that won the defenders' series in the 1995 America's Cup. Sclavounos used a sophisticated program called SWAN (Ship Wave ANalysis) to test Giles' design in every sort of sea condition at speeds from 30 to 50 knots, simulating the water resistance, heave and pitch FastShip would experience. The program found that the water resistance the revolutionary hull generated was less than that typical of existing naval or mercantile ships, and comparable to that of a highly sophisticated America's Cup yacht. The combination of Giles' fine bow and wide but shallow stern generated very little additional resistance at high speeds, while FastShip's planned length – a minimum of 230 metres at the water-line – will give her an additional advantage: because she is longer than the gap between most Atlantic waves, heave and pitch will be minimized. So the sceptics' doubts may yet be proved to be unfounded.

'The great technical issue is whether the ship can maintain her speed in high seas,' Sclavounos explained. 'And the art of the challenge is that speed is not only something which is desirable from a purely economic point of view, but is also the means of overcoming the power of the sea. FastShip is actually designed to benefit from the power because it will travel a level course rather than pitch. This ship, I think, is a marvellous harmony.'

■ **PRECIOUS CARGOES** The most frequently heard criticism of FastShip is that she is being built to meet a demand that does not actually exist. An extra day or two in transit is insignificant, it is argued, compared to the enormous cost of ensuring a faster service.

The FastShip team is certain that this argument is wrong. For the last half-century, anyone shipping freight from one continent to another has generally sent small, high-value items expensively by air and larger ones slowly but relatively cheaply by sea. The difference in delivery time can be dramatic: priority air freight moves between Europe and the United States in under three days, including the time needed to clear customs and travel to and from the air termini, while the cheapest sea freight can take thirty-five days to make the same journey. But the high cost of air freight has prevented it from ever gaining more than a minuscule proportion of the total market. Even now, with all the hundreds of thousands of kilometres flown each day, 99 per cent of intercontinental freight is moved by ship.

There is obvious potential for Giles to capture some of the cargo currently crossing the Atlantic by air. However, the tiny volume of transatlantic air freight – some 1.6 million tons each year – means that FastShip could capture the entire market and still have capacity to spare. Clearly Giles will also have to make significant inroads into the sea freight market, and here his targets are the so-called High Value Time Sensitive products – everything from cars, chemicals and electrical goods to fashion clothing – that are too bulky to be sent affordably by air, but too valuable to be allowed to sit waiting for a cheap sea-crossing. The FastShip consortium also expects to carry fresh food and drink.

Giles' initial plan calls for the construction of four vessels which will combine to provide a thrice-weekly service fifty-two weeks of the year. Each ship will carry 100 times more freight than the cargo version of the Boeing 747 and be more efficient than either aircraft or conventional container vessels. Despite the constant heavy demands on her engines, each FastShip should require a major service only once every twenty-four months and steam 8000 operational hours each year, compared to the 3500 hours a well-maintained cargo jet might fly in twelve months and the maximum of 3400 hours a container ship might spend at sea.

However, FastShip by herself will not be enough to guarantee a quick and reliable service. To compete with air freight and offer significant advantages over conventional sea freight, loading and unloading will have to be rapid. The ship's turnaround time must also be kept to a minimum if she is to work to her planned schedule and repay her costs; and trans-shipment to road or rail services will have to be swift and smooth. This problem has presented the FastShip team with new and significant engineering challenges that have nothing to do with ship design.

Traditional container ships are unloaded by crane. The containers are stacked on the dock, and later moved on to lorries or trains. FastShip plans a far more efficient roll-on, roll-off (ro-ro) service, like a ferry. Instead of unloading containers one by one by crane, whole 'crocodiles', stacked two high, will leave the ship through double-deck stern doors on high-tech air pads which work on the hovercraft principle. A set of four linked pads can be combined to make a so-called 'flow-flow' platform big enough to support two 12 metre containers, which can then be loaded and unloaded far more quickly than by crane. A pilot air pad system known as Alicon – Air-Lift Container – has already been set up at the Swedish port of Gothenburg, and Giles is confident that all the 9200 tons of freight a FastShip can carry could be disembarked in four to six hours, compared to the forty-eight it takes to unload a typical large container ship using cranes. Again, this system is the subject of an international patent application by Thornycroft Giles. The huge size of FastShip's stern doors means that it will even be possible to load one side of the ship at the same swift rate while unloading the other, further cutting an already rapid turnaround time.

■ **ONWARD TO THE PACIFIC** With solutions to most major technical problems in hand, Giles' major challenge now is to raise the money to build his first fast ship. United States government funds are expected to meet almost 90 per cent of the cost, not least because the military is interested in FastShip's potential to carry supplies and reinforcements rapidly to any trouble spot. Volvo, the Swedish car manufacturer, is involved too. The company has calculated that an efficient FastShip service to the United States via Zeebrugge in Belgium could substantially cut costs and inventory and perhaps even make it unnecessary to maintain a manufacturing capacity in America. The port of Philadelphia is also interested. Philadelphians failed to modernize their facilities in the 1980s and, as a result, lost the vital transatlantic container trade. They have responded by spending $200 million on raising the clearance of every railway bridge between the docks and the city limits so that tracks can be used by trains carrying the double decks of containers that FastShip will unload. With this sort of backing, Giles hopes to lay down his first keel in 1996 and launch two years later. If he can keep to this schedule, FastShip could go into service in 1998 with the aim of eventually taking between 5 and 7 per cent of the transatlantic freight market – and offer her backers a highly satisfactory 40 per cent return on their investment. The next step would be to conquer the Pacific by running freight thrice-weekly from Japan to the West Coast of America and trans-shipping some of the cargo by rail across the continent to another FastShip waiting at Philadelphia. A voyage that took the swiftest tea clipper three months to complete could thus be made in less than two weeks.

CHAPTER SIX

FAR

Scorched grit and dust spiralled around the heads of a line of soldiers as they shovelled soil and sweated in the oven of an Egyptian summer. Around them, makeshift earthworks zig-zagged across the Nile delta, blocking the path of an unseen enemy. It was 1799 and Napoleon's perspiring army of the Orient was building a fort near the little village of Rosetta.

They dug, until one private's spade clanked against a large, black stone. He bent to scoop the earth away from the rock and exposed a ragged piece of polished black basalt the size of a small table-top. It was blank on one side, but the other bore the remnants of a lengthy inscription in three tongues. The bottom one was Greek and revealed that the carving had been made in 196 BC. The others were translations of the Greek text into two hitherto undeciphered scripts: demotic, the common language of ancient Egypt, and hieroglyphic.

The savants who had accompanied Napoleon were beside themselves with excitement at this discovery. They recognized that they had in their possession a key that could unlock all the thousands of inscriptions that had lain unread in Egypt since the secret of hieroglyphic had been lost early in the Christian era; and so it proved. A linguistic prodigy named Jean François Champollion eventually succeeded in deciphering the script. The whole brilliant story of the pharaohs tumbled out, and with it came the earliest history of mankind.

Now, two centuries later, the story of the Rosetta stone has inspired another project, one with a still more ambitious goal – an understanding not just of the history of man, but of time and space. The key to this mystery lies not in the baking sands of Egypt, but more than 440 million kilometres away in the unimaginable cold of deep space, on the surface of an unremarkable comet called Wirtanen.

Rosetta is the name given to perhaps the most daring space shot since the moon landings – an attempt by America's National Aeronautics and Space Administration (NASA) and the European Space Agency (ESA) to land a tiny spacecraft on a comet and drill down into its surface to sample, and then analyse, the substance from which it is made. The mission is not scheduled to launch until 2003 and even then it will take a further nine years for the craft to reach Wirtanen and report its findings back to Earth. The wait will be worth it, though. If Rosetta is a success it will answer a question that has been puzzling astronomers for centuries: what, exactly, are

Previous page: Halley's comet; its most recent close encounter with Earth was in 1986.

comets made from? And the results should yield clues as to how our solar system, and perhaps the universe itself, were formed.

■ DEEP SPACE HANDICAP RACE The Rosetta project has been on ESA's drawing boards for many years. It was originally intended to be a sample-return mission, a 'crash-and-grab' that would end with a probe taking off from the surface of a comet and flying back to Earth with its precious contents. This was ruled to be too expensive and the idea now is to land one or two automated probes that will contain miniature laboratories capable of carrying out analyses and beaming the results back home. Rosetta Mark Two will cost half as much money as the Mark One version – but generate twice as many problems for the project's engineers.

The men who are expected to make everything possible face a phenomenal

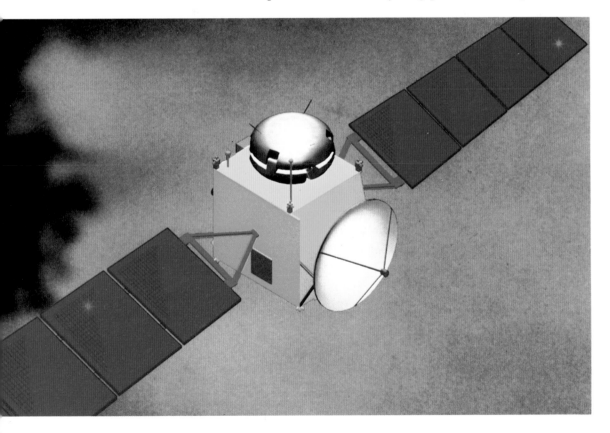

An artist's impression of the planned Rosetta space probe. The craft – scheduled to be launched in 2003 – will carry a miniature lander to comet Wirtanen and relay an analysis of a core sample from its surface back to Earth.

challenge. Wirtanen is a practically invisible pinprick travelling through an endless vacuum. And even if the rendezvous is successful Rosetta will have to land on an unknown surface – the comet could be made of anything from deep-frozen, solid rock to fluffy 'cosmic shaving cream' – extend a robotic auger and drill a metre down into the unknown. Then it will have to extract a few crumbs of matter, transfer them back into the body of the landing craft to analyse what they contain, and transmit its findings home. All this must be done by a lander clinging to a comet tearing through space at a speed of 30 kilometres per second – more than 100 times faster than a speeding bullet – and working in microgravity in cryogenic temperatures down to 200°C below zero. There are strict financial limits, too; budgets are tight and there is no question of sending a large, sophisticated robot to do the work. The robotic drill must weigh no more than a bag of potatoes, and the nuclear batteries that will power the Rosetta craft will deliver less electricity than the light bulb in a refrigerator.

Two men, from different engineering backgrounds and working on different continents, are competing to design the sampling system that will be deployed on Wirtanen. One is Stephen Gorevan, a shock-haired, bespectacled American who runs a company called Honeybee Robotics in New York. The other is Mauro Fenzi, a smartly dressed young scientist from Milan who works for Tecnospazio, a slightly larger, better resourced but more diverse Italian company. Fenzi was involved in ESA's planned sample-return mission, and has spent six years of his life working towards the goal of extracting a sample from a comet. Gorevan is a comparative newcomer who learned of the project only by chance and had little more than a year to catch up. Both men badly want the Rosetta contract, but each has to recognize that, in the end, the decision as to which of their designs hitches a ride into history depends as much on the politics of their business as it does on the ingenuity and reliability of their sampling equipment.

The competition between the two parties is fierce not just because the challenges of the mission make it attractive, but also because Rosetta has acquired

Stephen Gorevan is designing an automatic sampling device to carry out one of the most difficult tasks in the history of space exploration: extracting a core from a nucleus that could be made of anything from 'cosmic shaving cream' to granite.

the reputation of being a project 'with legs'. Space research is no longer as lavishly funded as it was in the days of the Apollo programme, and many projects are modified or even cancelled long before they blast off. Opportunities to engineer a system that has an excellent chance of being put into operation are increasingly rare, and the proposed co-operation between Europe and the United States – with Europe providing most of the funds, the rocket and an orbiter, and the United States the lander – gives the Rosetta mission the best possible chance of going ahead.

There will be co-operation, too, between the engineers working on the lander and their senior partners, the scientists in charge of the project. The scientists' first job is to place the Rosetta probe alongside Wirtanen, but this is actually one of the more straightforward parts of the mission. Landing a 45 kilogram capsule on the surface of the comet is a tougher challenge: the immediate problem will be to prevent it bouncing straight off again. Missions to the moon, Venus and Mars have relied on gravity to hold their landers in place; Wirtanen, which is just a few kilometres in diameter, has practically none, so the Rosetta lander – fittingly named Champollion – will probably be equipped with three or four fragile legs designed to collapse on impact and allow anchoring devices to engage and grip the surface.

Once Champollion is safely on the comet, scientists at ESA's Mission Control will signal it to commence work. Both Gorevan and Fenzi have decided that the auger must be powered in order to drill down from the main body of the lander into the unknown substance of the comet's nucleus – in microgravity it will not simply drop down until it makes contact with the surface. But how much more power, if any, will be required to penetrate the nucleus remains a mystery. 'We will be in cryogenic temperatures,' Fenzi said, 'in a vacuum and possibly surrounded by a lot of dust. We could encounter very hard stone or something else; we have to prepare for a wide range of possibilities and that's why it's very, very difficult to know how much force will be required.'

Gorevan has also anticipated this nightmare. 'It's difficult to be involved in a situation like this, because I like to be able to define a problem so I can solve it,' he explained. 'To an engineer, the unknown is like a silver spike to a vampire. How are we going to design a penetration system to go into something that can't be defined? Well, there's probably a way to do it, but it doesn't leave me with a very comfortable feeling in my stomach.'

Just to complicate matters, every contingency has to be planned for many years in advance. Gorevan admits to a recurring nightmare in which he realizes, years into the mission and with Rosetta part of the way to Wirtanen, that some vital component has been forgotten and the whole project has become a multi-million pound fiasco. In reality, he concedes, such a total failure is unlikely, but it is certainly possible that the drilling operation will be only partially successful. The lander may find itself positioned over a fissure, for example, where its metre-long auger can drill only a few centimetres into the actual surface of the comet. Or a sudden change in consistency – possibly as the drill moves from dust to solid rock – may prove too much for the computer program controlling the drilling.

Such potential problems make automating the sampling operation a significant challenge in itself. The Rosetta mission will be of short duration – the auger will drill for no more than a few hours – so there will be little opportunity for engineers on Earth to influence what happens. Instead, on-board sensors will measure depth, thrust and torque (the rotational thrust imparted to the drilling action) and regulate the power necessary to complete the operation. If resistance is low, thrust alone should be sufficient to retrieve a sample; if the probe encounters a harder surface, torque will be added; and if torque reaches levels that threaten to send the lander spinning crazily around the axis of its auger, power will be increased to control it.

The limited power available means that both Honeybee and Tecnospazio have had to invest considerable thought in puzzling out how to penetrate the widest possible variety of potential surfaces. Honeybee started its programme by buying dry ice – the simplest, cheapest approximation of what Wirtanen's surface layer may resemble – and taking a hand drill to it to get some idea of the best drills and augers to employ. Bits that passed this initial trial were subjected to more rigorous examination in baths of liquid nitrogen, where their torque and thrust were measured in the $-200°C$ temperatures they will encounter in deep space. The same tests gave Gorevan a good idea of whether there would be real difficulty in obtaining a sample at cryogenic temperatures.

Mauro Fenzi, Gorevan's rival, is pinning his hopes on a miniature robotic arm that will transfer samples into a tiny laboratory within the body of the probe. The electricity available is less than that required to power a light-bulb.

One limit that emerged during these early experiments was the problem of isolating the sample from the auger and ensuring that its temperature is raised by no more than a degree or two as it is extracted from the comet's surface. If it warms significantly it may discharge gases and lose some of its constituents. The solution was to propose a super-insulated chamber within the auger in which a sample can be sealed, and to limit the drilling operation to very low-speed work. High-speed drills heat up quickly – and also need too much power.

What happens, though, if the auger has to penetrate material far harder than dry ice? Here the best solution seemed to be one familiar to anyone who has dabbled in do-it-yourself: add a hammer action to the drill. Future experiments will seek to determine how many blows the drill will need to strike per minute and whether there will be enough power available for it to draw on. Even if there is, engaging the hammer action will be a last resort. There is a real danger that the percussive impacts may dislodge Champollion from the surface of the comet and send it tumbling away into space.

Both contenders have broadly similar schemes for acquiring a sample: use a hollow auger to drill down and then, at a pre-set depth, move the tip of the drill bit to expose a small cavity inside. Once the sample has been obtained the tip can be retracted to its start position, sealing the cometary material before returning it to the lander. However, even if the auger successfully penetrates a full metre below the surface of Wirtanen, the Rosetta mission's engineering problems will have only just begun. Deciding how to transfer and analyse the sample is an equally tricky puzzle, and it is here that Gorevan's and Fenzi's approaches differ most significantly.

Fenzi plans to call on some of the engineering expertise already developed at Tecnospazio to install a small robotic arm, some 40 centimetres long and weighing 1.2 kilograms, inside the lander. The prototype arm is equipped with pincers that would pick up the sample container and transfer it to instruments that would analyse its contents. It is a complex piece of equipment that would require Champollion to carry additional sensors and circuit boards, but Fenzi is certain that this is the best and most efficient way of carrying out a vital task. Gorevan fears the arm adds unnecessary complexity and weight to the probe; Honeybee prefers the far simpler idea of moving the whole sample, still inside its insulating chamber, to a position adjacent to the 'ovens' in which the analysis would take place.

'We've been in the robot business for thirteen years and we know how hard it is to make a flexible, simple robot that's lightweight,' Gorevan said. 'But sometimes I wake up and wonder if they are doing it exactly right and I'm completely wrong.'

Both engineers agree that simplicity will be one of the keys to a successful mission; it translates not just into reliability but also into cost-effectiveness. In any case, the encounter with Wirtanen will take place so far away that it would take 45 minutes for remote control instructions to reach the lander and for its responding signals to be received back on Earth. Detailed control of the operation will therefore not be a practical option. Instead, the whole mission may well depend on designing a machine in which the fewest possible number of things can go wrong.

Gorevan explained: 'We have only one chance to do this, and we want to make sure we haven't relied on unduly complex systems. So we don't depend on sophisticated sensors to align two pieces of equipment; instead we'll have simple switches and mechanical interlocks. We'll design two shapes that can move along each other until they fit perfectly together.'

Finally, the two rivals have to worry about the problems that come with any one-shot international mission. Fenzi is concerned about handling the project's scientists: 'As usual, they will want to do a lot of things without thinking about the technical problems.' For Gorevan, the real challenge will lie in taking space-probe technology a single huge step forward. 'We have to solve every problem right off the bat,' he warns. 'It's as though we were a relay team preparing for the Olympics who were not allowed to compete before the final race – just training, training, training in the gym and on our own private track. No practice competitions – just straight into the Olympic stadium. And we have to come back with a medal.'

■ **THE LONG-HAIRED ONES** The Rosetta project matters because comets, some of the oldest and most mysterious objects in our galaxy, may hold the key to our understanding of the universe – and because they have long exercised a powerful sway over human imagination. Ancient inscriptions and astronomical records show that their advent was regarded as significant by every early civilization, generally because they were thought to be harbingers of change. A comet may have put paid to the dinosaurs. The Romans and the Chinese carefully recorded the appearances of these celestial heralds and speculated as to their significance. Halley's comet, the most famous of them all, blazed over Normandy as William the Conqueror was preparing for his invasion of England. Giotto painted it in 1301 and comets announced the First Crusade and the Spanish invasion of Peru. As late as 1910, when Halley reappeared over the United States, an Oklahoma group calling themselves the Sacred Followers prepared to sacrifice a virgin to appease it. They were prevented from carrying through their plan only by the arrival of the police.

The word 'comet' is itself of great antiquity; it comes from ancient Greek and is derived from a word meaning 'long-haired one'. And it was the Greeks who formed some of the first theories to explain what these fiery visitors were and where they came from. Writing nearly three centuries before the birth of Christ, Aristotle posited a cosmos which was centred on an immobile Earth surrounded by nine concentric spheres. Each of the first seven contained one of the major heavenly bodies then known, from the moon out to Saturn. An eighth contained the stars, and the ninth was an empty 'prime mover' that caused the other spheres to rotate around our planet. At the edge of our atmosphere, the sage continued, were 'windy exhalations' from the Earth which, when set ablaze by the motions of the rotating spheres beyond, appeared as comets, shooting stars or swirling galaxies.

Aristotle's theories were destined to enjoy an extraordinary popularity. Though he was a philosopher rather than an astronomer, his views on the cosmos held sway long into the Christian era. Indeed, it was not until the sixteenth century that a Danish astronomer, Tycho Brahe, suggested that comets might be celestial objects moving around the sun. Brahe, a mild eccentric who dressed up in magician's robes in preparation for an evening at his telescope and wore a false nose fashioned of gold in place of the one he had lost in a duel, believed that comets revolved between Venus and Earth and even suggested, correctly, that they might move in elliptical (rather than circular) orbits. Further progress was made a century later, when an unusually bright comet that appeared in 1682 attracted the attention of a British natural philosopher named Edmond Halley. Halley fell under the object's spell and spent long and fruitless hours attempting to plot its track across the heavens. Later he collated hundreds of historical records of comets in a search for patterns that might suggest that they had orbits and did not travel in straight lines across Earth's path and onwards into the void, never to be seen again. Reviewing his work, he thought he could identify a comet reported in 1661 with one described in 1532;

and that his own comet of 1682 was a body seen every 575 years and dated back at least as far as 44 BC, when it had appeared in the heavens to mourn the death of Julius Caesar.

Halley's identifications were wrong, but he was on the right track. He finally persuaded himself that the comet of 1682 was identical to one that had previously been noted in 1607 and before that in 1531. In 1705 he predicted, on this basis, a further reappearance in 1758, seventy-six years on from 1682. All that fateful year astronomers scanned the heavens in the hope of being the first to report the comet's return, but for more than eleven months nothing was seen. Some were beginning to express doubts about Halley's theory when from Dresden in central Europe the news came that Johann Georg Palitzsh – a farmer by day and a keen amateur astronomer by night – had seen a pinprick of light in the sky in the position predicted. The wanderer had returned, as it would do again in 1835, 1910 and 1985. This time it was given a name: Halley's comet.

Edmond Halley's work established that comets do indeed rush through the solar system in more or less regular orbits, but did little to answer two intriguing questions: where do they come from, and what are they made of? The first problem was not resolved to the satisfaction of most astronomers until 1950 when Jan Oort, a Dutch astronomer, published an acclaimed paper that set out a new way of explaining the workings of the solar system. Oort hypothesized that way beyond Pluto there exists a primordial swarm of innumerable comets – perhaps 100 000 million of them, albeit with a collective mass less than that of Earth – that are slowly orbiting the sun at distances of up to two light years – half-way to Proxima Centauri, the star nearest to our solar system. His theory had an immediate appeal to astronomers, who named the swarm the Oort Cloud in his honour. Very occasionally, it is now believed, some of its members have their orbits disrupted by a rogue star that comes hurrying through the galaxy and into the cloud. Yanked from their orbits by the visitor's immense gravitational pull, some of the comets are pushed into paths that eventually take them into the solar system and within sight of Earth. Sometimes they are even captured by the gravity of the planets they pass (Pluto's large moon, Chiron, is thought to have once been a comet), and sometimes gravity draws them into a planet's path until they collide with it. Such collisions generally involve tiny, practically invisible comets which are broken up by friction as they

Halley's comet is one of the brightest and certainly the best known of the comets visible from Earth. Its visitations have been recorded as portents throughout history and in 1910 one Oklahoma group attempted to sacrifice a virgin to appease it.

encounter the upper atmosphere, causing no damage. Very occasionally, however – perhaps once every 500 years or so, perhaps no more than once in 10 000 years, for the periodicity is disputed – Earth encounters larger beasts.

■ **THE FIRE CAME BY** The most recent significant collision between Earth and an object from the void occurred at dawn on 30 June 1908, near the Stony Tunguska River in a remote and – fortunately – sparsely populated area of Siberia. Passengers on a Trans-Siberian railway train rumbling through the town of Kansk were jolted awake at 7.17 a.m. by a roar as the object shot overhead, glowing a fiery blue from its encounter with the atmosphere. A shock wave that preceded the invader rattled and shook the train so severely that its driver brought it screeching to a halt for fear it would be derailed.

The object never reached the surface. It appears to have disintegrated while still some 8500 metres above the ground in an explosion heard 650 kilometres away, the equivalent of detonating a 12.5 megaton hydrogen bomb. Seismographs in Java and Washington DC registered the shock as a sizeable earthquake; closer to the point at which the detonation occurred Siberian reindeer herdsmen were deafened by the blast. Merchants at the trading post of Vanavera, 65 kilometres away, had to shield their faces from its fierce heat. Seconds later the shock wave arrived, shattering windows and tearing apart huts and houses. Closer still to the epicentre, huge swathes of virgin pine forest were flattened: the tree trunks fell away from the centre of the blast to form a convenient signpost for the expeditions that would eventually trek through the wilderness to search for evidence of an impact. Over the Tunguska valley a pillar of cloud, perhaps 20 kilometres high, boiled upwards filling the air with a swirling mass of soil and debris that fell later as sinister black rain. Days later the after-effects of the detonation were still being witnessed. Yellow and orange lights danced in the skies over Berlin and London, Copenhagen and Vienna; and in Antwerp, after sunset, the northern horizon appeared to be on fire.

The remoteness of the Siberian wastes, and the intervention of the First World War and the Russian Revolution, seriously delayed scientific investigation of the so-called Tunguska Event. It was 1927 before a Soviet expedition led by a mineralogist, Leonard Kulik, penetrated the area. The Soviets' interest in what had exploded over Tunguska was scientific, but there were also commercial considerations to address. Earlier in the 1920s an American mining firm had commenced drilling work at Meteor Crater, Arizona, an immense pockmark in the earth's skin some 1200 metres (3900 feet) wide and 175 metres (570 feet) deep. Some 420 metres (1370 feet) down their drills hit a solid seam of oxidized meteoric iron which was 93 per cent pure but contained traces of valuable platinum and iridium. The seam proved to be too deeply buried to be worth mining, but if the Tunguska object also turned out to have been a meteor it was possible that a valuable resource could be dug out of the Siberian swamps.

Guided by the thousands of bleak, branchless tree trunks that still lay scattered where they had fallen in 1908, the members of Kulik's expedition trudged north through the Siberian spring. Hacking their way with painful slowness through the wilderness, they came to an area where the upper portions of the trees were charred by fire and, finally, to a place where some trunks had survived the blast and still stood upright, though burned black. This, Kulik believed, was the epicentre of a blast which had stripped all the branches and foliage from the trees beneath it but which, because it had struck them directly from above, had failed to fell their slim trunks.

The team spread out to search for signs of meteoric impact. It was a thankless task. The area was a morass of bogs and stagnant pools, any one of which might have been a water-filled crater. Kulik himself suspected that a large marshy area he named the Great Cauldron might hide the remains of a single large meteor. But there was no evidence to back this hypothesis. The expedition could only find a number of strange shallow holes, ranging in size from a metre or two to dozens of metres across, which resembled no known meteor impact site. There were, it became apparent, no riches to be dug out of the boggy soil.

If the Tunguska object was not an ordinary meteor, what was it? Setting aside the more esoteric theories that have been advanced since Kulik's expedition – that a miniature black hole, a particle of anti-matter or even an alien spacecraft had crashed into Earth – the most logical explanation seems to be that a small comet had entered the atmosphere undetected and broken up over Siberia. And the lack of evidence for impact sites is perhaps a clue. Could it be that the comet's main constituents were not iron and nickel, but something else – something like ice?

■ **DIRTY SNOWBALLS** Tycho Brahe had his own ideas about what comets were made of. He suggested that they were the 'exhalations' of planets spat somehow into space. Johann Kepler, the great seventeenth-century German astronomer, disagreed. He thought comets were formed spontaneously in the 'celestial air' by a mysterious process he named 'thickening'. Galileo, Kepler's Italian contemporary, guessed they might be no more than reflected sunlight and others believed they were slag thrown out by sunspots, or pure fire travelling through space. In the years

Comets are among some of the most mysterious objects in our galaxy and early civilizations saw them as harbingers of change. Modern scientists believe that they may hold the key to how the universe was formed.

immediately after the Tunguska Event, however, another theory of cometary origin held sway, one based on detailed observations of Halley's comet when it appeared in 1910.

Halley is the brightest of the sixteen comets in relatively tight orbits around the sun which regularly and predictably pass Earth and is therefore an ideal object for study. In 1910 a group of American astronomers sailed to Hawaii in order to watch from the most favourable possible position as it crossed the face of the sun. They hoped to see a silhouette of the comet's nucleus – and would have done so if it had been nearly as massive as some contemporary experts believed. Even an object a thousandth of the size of the moon would have been visible through the astronomers' telescopes, but nothing whatsoever was seen. It seemed, therefore, that the nucleus might be little more than a loose collection of dust – a sort of cosmic hailstorm of meteors just waiting to fall behind their companions into the slightly less dense tail of the comet, and thence out into their own lonely orbits.

An alternative theory of the origin of comets emerged in 1950 championed by one of the best-respected members of the rather small group of astronomers interested in the subject: Fred Whipple, a director of the Smithsonian Museum's Astrophysical Observatory. He was becoming convinced that comets were solid objects – 'dirty snowballs' made of lumps of meteoric material and ice coated with grime which, warmed by an approach to the sun, spewed out gas and dust particles that gave the nucleus its blazing glow and formed its equally characteristic tail.

Whipple's theory was merely a restatement of an older notion of comets and since its publication his views have been expanded and elaborated by other astronomers. Observations made through infra-red telescopes, and calculations based on reflectivity, suggest that with some exceptions – the largest known comet, Sarabat, appears to have been about 300 kilometres across early in its life – most observable examples have nuclei between 2 and 6 kilometres in diameter. Typical comets rotate rapidly, propelled it seems by jets of gas from their interiors; most complete a revolution around the sun within a few hours or days. Studies of their reflectivity also show that many are remarkably dark. They reflect only half as much light as black paper, for example, which places them amongst the darkest bodies in the solar system. This suggests that cometary snowballs must be extremely dirty, perhaps covered by insulating blankets of dust many centimetres, or even metres, thick through which gases escape by way of pores in the surface. Many examples, including Halley, are shaped like rugby balls, or potatoes. Some, perhaps those that are close to disintegration, seem to be thin and disc-shaped.

The great merit of Whipple's theory was that it laid to rest a number of anomalies about comets which had been puzzling astronomers for years. It accounted for their ability to produce gas at a remarkable rate and explained why those that pass near the sun, as Halley does, do not disintegrate altogether at perihelion – their closest approach to the star. Most excitingly, however, it gave engineers and scientists a new target: if comets really were dirty snowballs it should be possible to land on one and settle the issue of their origin once and for all. As the 1950s gave way to the new space age of the 1960s and 1970s, the techniques that would be needed on such a mission were tried on targets closer to home. The Soviets and the Americans began to use space probes to gather and analyse samples from the surface of the moon, Venus and Mars.

■ **SHAVING THE MAN IN THE MOON** The Americans' chief concern in their attempts to recover rock and dust samples was to locate a safe area on the moon where they could land a manned spacecraft. Without the data these missions would provide they could not be certain that a landing would be possible. The moon might be made of rock but, according to one theory, its crust could be covered with layers of dust so thick a spacecraft would settle into them and disappear.

The research programme that NASA set in train in the 1950s was so ambitious it caused the agency anxiety for years. Ranger 3, the first probe planned actually to crash on to the moon, was equipped with television cameras to beam back photographs of the surface during its descent, a spectrometer to measure electromagnetic radiation and an extremely sensitive seismometer designed to detect whether the moon was subject to dangerous tremors caused by the impact of meteorites. Considerable ingenuity was employed to ensure that the seismometer – which, if all went well, would become the first machine to transmit data back from the surface of any of the planets and satellites in the solar system – would land intact and be deployed correctly. Because Ranger was programmed to smash into the moon at a speed of more than 9600 kilometres per hour, the delicate instrument would have to be ejected in a separate lander as the main probe began its final descent.

Parachutes were useless – the moon has no atmosphere – so the seismometer capsule was fitted with retrorockets to slow its impact speed to a mere 320 kilometres per hour. In order to absorb the still substantial shock of the landing, 20 centimetres of balsa wood was packed around the capsule and its interior was filled with a thick oil. After landing, two bullets would be fired automatically from inside the capsule, the holes allowing the oil to seep away and leaving the seismometer, mounted on springs, ready to begin its work.

The **Surveyor series of moon probes brought success to NASA after years of failure. Here the trellis-like robotic arm of Surveyor 3** scrapes at the surface during soil sampling experiments in **April 1967. Information from Surveyor finally** convinced the **Americans it would** be safe to set a manned spacecraft down on the moon.

In the event, this careful planning went to waste in a protracted series of almost farcical mishaps. Instead of crashing on to its intended target, Ranger 3 missed it by 37 000 kilometres. Ranger 4, which followed in April 1962, impacted correctly but did so on the dark side of the moon where contact with Earth was impossible. Ranger 5 suffered a total power failure shortly after take-off. At this point NASA decided that the seismographical part of the programme was over-complex and scrapped it, leaving Ranger 6 to concentrate on photographing possible landing sites. The lessons of the previous three missions had been learned by the time this probe blasted off in January 1964. It crashed into the surface close to the point at which it had been aimed, with all its three television cameras switched on. Unfortunately, the command that activated them had been accidentally transmitted early in the flight. The cameras obtained 40 000 useless pictures of empty space, and by the time Ranger 6 reached the moon its batteries had run down to the point where its signals were too weak to be received on Earth.

This expensive and lengthy series of failures disheartened NASA, but at least its craft had reached its destination. The Soviets, meanwhile, had successfully placed probes in orbit around the moon and photographed its dark side without appearing to attempt a landing. This policy now changed. A number of landers in the Lunik series crashed into the surface – whether deliberately or as part of a failed soft-landing attempt was not clear at the time – and in February 1966 a capsule ejected by Lunik 9 became the first probe to soft-land successfully on the moon.

The 100 kilogram capsule touched down in the Ocean of Storms and successfully used a panoramic camera to photograph the surrounding landscape. What is more important, perhaps, is that the success of its mission proved that at least parts of the surface would make suitable targets for a manned landing. Later in 1966 further Lunik probes orbited the moon, measured its magnetic and gravitational fields and carried out an aerial soil analysis. They reported that the surface appeared to be made of basaltic rock. Lunik 15 touched down on Christmas Eve that year and deployed instruments to measure the density and firmness of the soil.

It was not until the American Surveyor series of probes was under way that a lander actually took samples from the surface. Surveyors 1 and 2 were photographic missions. Their cameras pointed downwards to show close-ups of the landing area and revealed the site to be thinly covered with a fine dust. Surveyor 3 was much more ambitious: it carried a miniaturized laboratory and a robotic scoop with which to scrape at the lunar soil. It touched down in April 1967 and caused concern at Mission Control when it bounced on initial impact. Fortunately, the instruments on board escaped damage and the probe successfully lowered its light, trellis-like robotic arm to the surface. The arm scraped four shallow trenches and returned to the capsule with its scoop full of small rocks and moon dust. Inside the miniature laboratory, the samples were subjected to a series of tests that revealed their composition to include oxides, silicon, aluminium, calcium and iron, as well as magnesium, carbon and sodium – a mixture similar to that found in volcanic lava on Earth. These results were confirmed and amplified by three further probes. The Ranger and Surveyor missions had cleared the way for the Americans to attempt a manned landing on the moon.

■ **DRILL BITS ON THE MORNING STAR** The Apollo 11 lander and its crew of two astronauts touched down on the surface of the moon on 20 July 1969. By then, exploration of the other planets in the solar system had been under way for half a decade, albeit with little success. Venus, Earth's sister and the planet nearest to our own in size, was the first to receive the attentions of visitors. In December 1962 America's Mariner 2 flew past Venus and became Earth's first successful interplanetary probe in the process. And between 1961 and 1967 the Soviets tried no less than eleven times to penetrate the layers of cloud that shield the planet's mysterious surface from man's gaze. That programme would be enormously ambitious today; in the early 1960s it was at the limit – and in many respects well beyond the limit – of space technology. Seven of the Soviet craft failed to get off the launch pad and of the four that did, three suffered communications failures and could do no more than pass mutely by Venus at ranges varying from 24 000 to 100 000 kilometres. The eleventh probe, Venera 3, succeeded in penetrating the planet's cloudy veil but crashed on to the surface, also without transmitting useful information.

The central mystery of Venus – the planet's atmosphere and the sort of surface conditions it had created – remained unresolved. Contemporary opinion was broadly divided between those who hoped the surface might in some way resemble Earth's and those, the great majority, who forecast that the dense cloud cover would hold in heat and raise the atmospheric temperature to the point where the planet became an intolerable desert so hot that metal placed on its surface would melt.

The first spacecraft to penetrate the clouds and beam back information about the planet was Venera 4. Like Gorevan and Fenzi puzzling over the mysterious Wirtanen, the Soviets who designed Venera 4 had no real idea what conditions their probe might encounter. Some astronomers had predicted that Venus might be covered by oceans of some sort, so the capsule was designed to float; even a suggestion by the maverick British scientist Fred Hoyle – that Venus might actually be covered in oil – was taken into account. In the event, however, the project's engineers made one fatal mistake. They based the design of the Venera lander on unrealistically low estimates of the planet's atmospheric pressure and inadvertently ensured its destruction. The true pressure pushing down on Venus is enormous – 100 times what we are used to on Earth. Subjected to this intolerable strain, Venera 4 imploded during its descent and ceased its transmission when it was 25 kilometres above the surface.

The Soviet academicians did not immediately recognize what had gone wrong, and for a while they refused to acknowledge that their mission had failed. They knew that the last data had been beamed back from an altitude of 25 000 metres and suggested that their probe had landed on a vast plateau far above the natural surface of the planet and then, perhaps, toppled over so that its radio antennae were pointed away from Earth. The Soviets' failure to redesign the Venera lander meant that the next two missions, Venera 5 and Venera 6, met with the same fate as Venera 4 when they arrived in 1969. Both were partial successes, successfully transmitting data during their descent before contact was lost. However, it was another nineteen months before Venera 7 landed on the true surface of Venus and sent back detailed information on the appallingly hostile environment it had discovered – a planet cloaked, as was already known, in choking cloud, but also baked to a temperature of 280°C.

The Soviets returned to the morning star in the autumn of 1981 with two sampling probes: Venera 13 and Venera 14. A hazy, maddeningly indistinct film taken from one lander shows a drill equipped with what appears to be some sort of suction device descending slowly to the surface but, more than a decade later, it remains extremely difficult to piece together the details of how exactly the Russians succeeded in gathering a sample. Nevertheless, the Veneras certainly managed to extract a core of Venusian soil and return it to the body of the lander for analysis.

The Americans, meanwhile, had focused their attention elsewhere. Leaving Venus to their bitter rivals in the space race, they had chosen to deploy their own sampling devices on the surface of another planet: Mars.

■ **VIKINGS ON THE RED PLANET** More than Venus, more indeed than any other planet in the solar system, Mars has the power to fascinate. Unlike Venus, its atmosphere is thin – the pressure is one-twentieth that on Earth – and its surface cold; the temperature falls to $-125°C$ at the poles. The planet's axis is at present tilted about 24 degrees off its orbital plane, close to Earth's axial tilt, and it completes a revolution around that axis each 24 hours and experiences seasons as we do. Polar icecaps and signs of water erosion suggest that once, when the sun was bigger and hotter than now, Mars may have possessed a more bearable climate. In the nineteenth century the American astronomer Percival Lowell mapped an intricate system of 'canals' he had observed on the surface and painted a picture of a dying civilization on a dry and desolate planet eking out an existence with the help of stupendous irrigation works. Even when his theories were discredited, the idea that Mars might once have supported life remained plausible. It was even conceivable that some sort of microbe might still exist on the surface.

Once man had finally ventured into space, the red planet became a natural target for investigation. As early as 1961 a NASA team planned to put a craft into orbit around Mars, using a new Centaur rocket to lift a 1000 kilogram probe into space. But the kind of cut-backs and economies that limit Stephen Gorevan and Mauro Fenzi today are nothing new; the development programme fell behind schedule, an older, smaller Agena launcher was substituted for the Centaur and the weight of the equipment shrank by three-quarters. NASA had to build a television camera, tape recorder and scanning and transmission equipment on to the Agena's tiny platform as well as a power source sufficient to keep the probe in operation for nearly twelve months.

In the days before miniaturized circuitry and microcomputers this was an exceptional challenge, particularly as the probe, now named Mariner 4, would be the first ever to rendezvous successfully with Mars. But the new weight limit had positive benefits. NASA's engineers were forced to move away from the Russian concept of maintaining an Earth-like atmosphere inside a heavy, complex capsule. Instead, they built a probe capable of working in a vacuum in extreme temperatures. The new design was much more reliable and could function for long periods in deep space. The scarcity of resources also placed great emphasis on reliability. The direct consequence was that American space probes began to experience far fewer launch and in-flight failures than did those of the Soviets.

Mariner 4 reached Mars in July 1965, as planned, and beamed back pictures that showed the surface to be far more moon-like than had been expected. Huge craters billions of years old scarred the crust, suggesting that the planet had never enjoyed an atmosphere like Earth's or been covered by oceans; and the atmosphere itself proved to be so thin that any water on the surface would have vaporized instantly. But even these disappointing results did not dampen NASA's enthusiasm for further exploration of the red planet. The next mission, it was suggested, should be the opposite of the cheap and cheerful Mariner project and involve landing a huge, 22 700 kilogram robotic laboratory capable of conducting complex soil sampling and analysis work and detecting any microscopic life forms.

Although the cost of such a probe soon proved to be prohibitive, the idea of sampling the Martian soil was still considered a good one. The Soviets agreed, but their attempts to reach the planet resulted in repeated failure. It was left to the US Viking project, which involved a lander no bigger than a Volkswagen Beetle, to cross this next frontier in space. However, the new mission soon became intensely controversial within the scientific and engineering communities at NASA and its engineering contractor, the Jet Propulsion Laboratory at Pasadena. Data and photographs sent back by Mariner 4 and its successors in orbit around Mars had convinced many people that the planet's thin atmosphere, lack of water (the polar icecaps had turned out to be made of solid carbon dioxide – 'dry ice') and catastrophic vulnerability to bombardment by ultraviolet rays and other forms of radiation meant there was no longer any realistic hope of finding life on its surface. But the fiscal cut-backs and sense of exhaustion that followed the conclusion of the moon landing programme meant that both institutions required a high profile mission to rekindle public enthusiasm and loosen the nation's purse strings once again. Of all the Viking programme's possible missions – the options included geological and mineralogical surveys of the planet – a search for life on Mars was most likely to grip the imagination. Over the protests of many veterans of the space race, the Viking landers were therefore engineered specifically to detect the minutest signs of microscopic life in a handful of soil samples.

Viking contained a series of chambers capable of carrying out experiments. In one, dust from the surface would be mixed with a broth of water vapour, water and nutrients concocted on Earth in the hope of tempting any Martian microbes present

The trenches dug by Viking 1 enabled the probe to take soil samples from 30 centimetres beneath the surface of the red planet and place them in a laboratory where they were tested for any signs of life. The results were negative; even so, some scientists argued that fossil life-forms could exist deeper down in the soil.

into a feeding frenzy that could be detected by biochemical instruments inside the capsule. Another experiment would use only carbon dioxide and xenon radiation, mimicking the principal compound in the Martian atmosphere and the stimulus of sunlight. Meanwhile, an automated gas chromatograph/mass spectrometer (GCMS) would seek to locate any organic chemicals in the soil that could potentially combine to create life, using the chromatograph to isolate the compounds and the spectrometer to identify them precisely. Set down anywhere on Earth, a sensitive GCMS would detect a 'signature' of organic chemicals that signalled life. NASA hoped it would do the same on Mars.

To retrieve soil samples, engineers at the Jet Propulsion Laboratory designed a robotic scoop on a semi-automatic, semi-remote-control arm that could be extended from the lander and guided, by way of television pictures, between the small rocks known to litter the surface of Mars and into patches of soil and dust. The arm terminated in a disc from which a small serrated 'comb' projected down to scrape at the soil. The dust that was gathered would then be funnelled back into chambers in the arm and returned to the body of the lander.

Viking 1, the first of two landers, touched down on the planet on 20 July 1976 and almost immediately began to sample the surface in its immediate vicinity. Together with Viking 2, she took twenty-one scoops of Martian soil. Initial results seemed to suggest that reactions indicative of some form of life were occurring within the nutrient broth. However, as a wave of enormous excitement prepared to sweep through JPL, it was realized that these results were simply too good to be true. The reactions were chemical rather than biochemical, and resulted from the introduction of water to a soil that had never before encountered it. When the results of the GCMS experiments were received they showed that not a single organic molecule had been detected; Martian soil was more sterile than had ever been anticipated. Although carbon, the basic building block of life, is abundant in Mars' atmosphere, in its icecaps and (probably) in the meteorites that still strike it, minerals on its surface dust have been superoxidized in the course of their reaction with ultraviolet light arriving from the sun. Any carbons that do reach the soil are rapidly burned up in further chemical reactions in this most hostile of environments.

The Viking programme proved – insofar as samples extracted from the tiniest area of a large planet could ever prove – that no life exists on Mars today. But, by deploying scoops to sample only the surface dust, the lander failed to answer every question. The depth of the planet's superoxidized surface layer remains unknown; is it possible that some form of life could exist beneath it? And what of the evidence suggesting that, billions of years in the past, huge quantities of water spewed forth from beneath the surface to flood immense areas and gouge great canyons and gorges? Did microbes flourish then, but become extinct when Mars turned into a desert once again? If Viking had carried drilling equipment instead of a scoop, it might have found evidence of life in fossil form.

■ **ENCOUNTERS WITH A COMET** Rosetta will not be the first craft to chase a comet through the heavens. International Cometary Explorer (ICE), a blind, adapted American satellite, came within 8000 kilometres of comet Giacobini-Zinner in September 1985; and six months later, during Earth's most recent close encounter with Halley's comet, a veritable armada of spacecraft converged on the visitor in the hope of resolving some of the unanswered questions its presence posed. Each carried sensors and instruments to probe the comet's coma – the luminous gases that surround its nucleus – and tail for clues to its origin and nature. All scored notable successes and added significantly to the relatively little that was known about Halley. But, because no attempt was made to launch a mission to the nucleus itself, many problems remain tantalizingly unresolved.

Every nation with a presence in space – except the United States, whose proposed Halley mission became a victim of NASA cut-backs – took advantage of this once in a lifetime opportunity to call on the solar system's most famous guest. Leading the way were two Soviet craft, Vega 1 and Vega 2. They were instrumented with French and ESA help, aimed at Halley by way of Venus, the Soviets' favourite planet, and fitted with mass spectrometers, heat sensors and optical equipment. They were followed by two Japanese capsules – tiny Sakigake (Pioneer), less than one-twentieth Vega's size, and the slightly larger Suisei (Comet) – designed to measure Halley's interaction with the solar wind and the enormous cloud of hydrogen gas that surrounds it.

Vega 1 was the first craft to reach the comet. On 6 March 1986 it passed within 8900 kilometres of Halley's nucleus, photographed it and took samples of the dust grains in its bow wave. Vega 2 was close behind and even closer to the comet, and repeated and amplified its companion's work. Many of the Soviet experiments worked admirably, but the quality of the photographic images – the key to public acclaim if not scientific success – was poor. Vega 1's telescopic lens was out of focus and its sister's film was over-exposed. The Japanese probes, meanwhile, soared further off, at distances of 7 million kilometres and 150 000 kilometres respectively, and watched Halley for months rather than the few short hours preferred by the more daring Europeans.

The Russian and Japanese craft were only curtain-raisers for the undoubted flagship of the international Halley fleet: ESA's Giotto. The probe, named after the Italian artist who had depicted the comet in the early years of the fourteenth century, was the culmination of a decade of wrangling and co-operation between the agency's fifteen member nations. Like all ESA designs it was tiny – less than 3 metres by 2 metres, smaller than a modest bedroom. But it was also sophisticated and highly intricate. Behind a special shield designed to let it penetrate deep into the dusty storms of Halley's coma it carried ten different instruments, each with its own mission. They included a camera, three spectrometers to calculate the comet's make-up, two plasma analysers, a dust-impact counter and a machine for measuring 'energetic particles' thrown off by the nucleus. Every gram of Giotto's 960 kilogram mass – only a fraction of which was allocated to the instruments – was carefully husbanded, then parcelled out and fought over by the international cast of scientists.

The Giotto mission was a success by any standard. The tiny capsule blasted off from French Guiana in July 1985 and was guided in towards Halley eight months later, with the help of data from Vega 1, to pass within 600 kilometres of the comet's nucleus. It was a triumph of celestial navigation. Halley was moving at a speed of 270 000 kilometres per hour and Giotto had travelled 144 million kilometres to reach the meeting-point. If the probe had been a single minute late at its rendezvous, Halley would have been 4000 kilometres off and receding into the distance – too far away for some of the delicately calibrated instruments on board the capsule to have functioned properly. As it was, the comet and its suitor met as planned. Giotto chased the million kilometre bow wave that had been detected early by the Vega probes and arced through the comet's 20 million kilometre long tail on its way towards its nucleus.

Most of the instruments on the probe followed their programmed instructions,

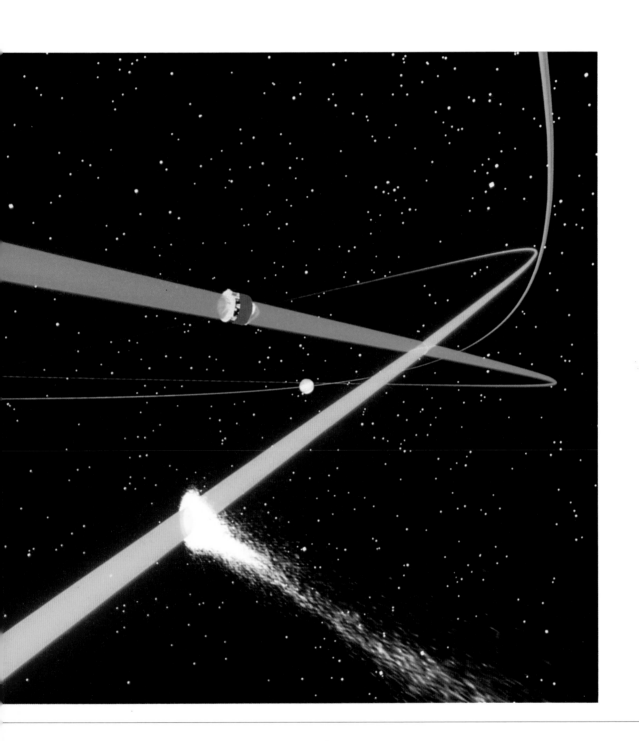

Trajectories for comet-intercept missions are complex. Here a European Space Agency simulation shows the orbit of **Earth in blue, the trajectory of the Giotto probe in green and the path of comet Grigg-Skjellerup, one of its targets, in orange.**

switched themselves off and on and searched the horizons for the information they required. But the vital camera was causing problems. The project team had earlier been forced to override part of the computer program that controlled it and they realized that this was causing confusion: the camera had decided that the comet was moving much faster than it was. If the error could not be corrected it would focus on empty space while the nucleus shot past and miss perhaps the greatest close-up opportunity of the space age.

Months and years of careful planning, of checking and re-checking calculations and of anticipating difficulties and allowing for them suddenly counted for nothing. If the problem was to be overcome, the program controlling the camera would have to be rewritten in a matter of a few hours. That meant working out what was going wrong, making the correct assumptions as to where Halley really was, adding a coda to the original program, and sending it off into space in time to catch the probe before its close encounter. Tension in ESA's cramped Mission Control rose unbearably; the stress became too much for one white-faced engineer, who had to be escorted from the room to recover. But an hour before the rendezvous the problem was finally resolved, new instructions were transmitted and the probe's camera shifted back on track.

As Giotto rushed through Halley's tail towards the mysterious nucleus, its dust shield was peppered by millions of particles thrown off into the coma. Each speck would have been potentially fatal to any normal space probe, but Giotto's shield not only protected its instruments from harm but actually acted as a cosmic scoop that collected data from each particle that smashed against the shield and fed it to the probe's spectrometers. Only once was Giotto thrown off course. As it closed on the nucleus one larger particle, weighing perhaps one-tenth of a gram, crashed into the shield at a speed of 2.7 million kilometres per hour, concussed the instruments and disrupted the probe's programmed spin. Twenty minutes' worth of crucial pictures and data from the closest phase of the approach was lost. The lesson for ESA is clear. The Rosetta mission craft will have to be exceptionally well shielded if it is to battle through Wirtanen's coma and land on the comet's dusty surface.

The international astronomical community was soon deluged with results from the cometary armada. First the American ICE probe detected unexpectedly large quantities of water molecules in the wake of comet Giacobini-Zinner, seeming to confirm Whipple's 'dirty snowball' theory. Then Vegas' and Giotto's close-up pictures of Halley were decoded. Two thousand images from the latter's camera alone revealed an unexpectedly complex body; the comet was larger, rougher and more active than anticipated. It was 15 kilometres long, as big as Manhattan, and although its surface was mostly ink-black, as expected, fissures suffused with brightness here and there spewed plumes of gas and dust into space. Much of the nucleus was chilled to temperatures of $-100°C$ but some parts were both active and hot enough to boil water. Chemical analyses showed that the nucleus and coma were full of carbons and carbon compounds including methane, ammonia and perhaps even formaldehyde – embalming fluid. But the greatest anomaly was that Halley did not seem to be quite the dirty snowball Whipple had predicted. It was craggy and cratered, and if ice was present it was not the comet's most prominent feature.

■ **COMETFALL** Only a mission such as the Rosetta project can answer the questions that Giotto posed. Only landing on a comet's surface and drilling into its nucleus can unveil its precise make-up. But Rosetta and its proposed landing craft, Champollion, could reveal far more than that. Analysis of the tarry carbon compounds that seem to exist on comets may well yield clues to how life evolved on Earth and how the solar system itself developed. If Oort's theory of cometary origin is correct, Wirtanen and its fellow visitors existed in the silent and unchanging void for billions of years before being deflected towards us; and in their nuclei they preserve matter as it was when our part of the galaxy was formed. They are moving, space-borne fossils that could tell us what the constituent elements of the solar system were at the first moment of its creation, and what their proportions were. And if Champollion succeeds in analysing the carbon compounds on Wirtanen, it may well discover that they contain some of the key building blocks of life on Earth. In other words, huge showers of comets may have created the water and carbon mixture necessary for life and sparked the very first steps in the billion-year evolution of the human race.

So don't ask Rosetta's engineers if their work matters. 'Its importance?' Gorevan asks. 'Well, it's an age-old thing. To be involved in such a momentous look at the origin of our solar system is a way of carving out a very tiny piece of immortality. And that's what we all seek, isn't it?'

Bailey, M.E. with Clube, S.V. and Napier, W.M., *The Origin of Comets*, Pergamon Press: Reed Book Services, 1990.

Brown, David, *Bridges: Three Thousand Years of Defying Nature*, Beazley, 1993.

Brunel's Tunnel ... and where it led, The Brunel Exhibition Project, 1980.

Calder, Nigel, *The Comet is Coming!*, Penguin, 1982.

Calder, Nigel, *Giotto to the Comets*, Presswork, 1992.

Campbell, George, *China Tea Clippers*, Adlard Coles, 1974.

Chapelle, Howard, *The Search for Speed Under Sail*, Allen & Unwin, 1968.

Corlett, Ewan, *The Iron Ship: the Story of the SS "Great Britain"*, Conway Maritime Press, 1990.

Edwards, I.E.S., *The Pyramids of Egypt*, Penguin 1991.

Gardiner, Robert (ed.), *Steam, Steel and Shellfire: the Steam Warship 1815-1905*, Conway Maritime Press, 1992.

Goldberger, Paul, *The Skyscraper*, Allen Lane, 1992.

Gunston, Bill, *Giants of the Sky: the Biggest Aeroplanes of All Time*, P.S.L., 1991.

Hopkins, Henry, *A Span of Bridges*, David & Charles, 1970.

Irving, Clive, *Wide Body: the Making of the 747*, Hodder, 1993.

James, Peter and Thorpe, Nick, *Ancient Inventions*, Michael O'Mara Books, 1995.

Lampe, David, *The Tunnel: The Story of the World's First Tunnel Under a Navigable River*, Harrap, 1963.

Levy, Matthys and Salvadori, Mario, *Why Buildings Fall Down: How Structures Fail*, W.W. Norton, 1994.

Lubbock, Basil, *The China Clippers*, Brown, 1919.

Mansfield, John, *Man on the Moon*, Constable, 1969.

McDonald, John, *Howard Hughes and His Hercules*, Airlife Publishing, 1983.

MacGregor, David, *The Tea Clippers: Their History and Development 1833-1875*, Conway Maritime Press, 1983.

Moorhouse, Geoffrey, *Imperial City: the Rise and Rise of New York*, Sceptre, 1989.

Murray, Bruce, *Journey Into Space: the First Three Decades of Space Exploration*, W.W. Norton, 1991.

Penn, Geoffrey, *Up Funnel, Down Screw! – the Story of the Naval Engineer*, Hollis & Carter, 1955.

Prebble, John, *The High Girders*, Penguin, 1979.

Reynolds, Donald, *The Architecture of New York*, Wiley, 1994.

Rolt, T.L.C., *Isambard Kingdom Brunel*, Penguin, 1990.

Salvadori, Mario, *Why Buildings Stand Up*, W.W. Norton, 1991.

Sandstrom, Gosta, *The History of Tunnelling: Underground Workings Through the Ages*, Barrie & Rockliff, 1963.

Selcrest, Meryl, *Frank Lloyd Wright*, Chatto, 1992. ·

Taylor, Michael and Hillman, Ellis, *London Under London: a Subterranean Guide*, John Murray, 1993.

Wallis, Shani, *Jubilee Line Extension: the Underground Perspective*, London, 1994.

West, Graham, *Innovation and the Rise of the Tunnelling Industry*, Cambridge University Press, 1988.

BIBLIOGRAPHY

INDEX

ENGINEERING AS A CAREER

If you wish to learn more about the engineering professions featured in *The Limit* you should contact the public relations department of the following organizations:

The Institution of Civil Engineers
One Great George Street
London SW1P 3AA

Tel 0171 222 7722

The Institution of Electrical Engineers
Savoy Place
London WC2R 0BL

Tel 0171 240 1871

The Institution of Mechanical Engineers
1 Birdcage Walk
London SW1H 9JJ

Tel 0171 222 7899

The Royal Aeronautical Society
4 Hamilton Place
London W1V 0BQ

Tel 0171 499 3515

Other queries may be directed to:

The Engineering Council
10 Maltravers Street
London WC2R 3ER

Tel 0171 240 7891